Farewell the Ivory Tower

J. A. CORRY

Farewell the Ivory Tower

UNIVERSITIES IN TRANSITION

McGILL–QUEEN'S UNIVERSITY PRESS

MONTREAL AND LONDON 1970

© McGill-Queen's University Press 1970
International Standard Book Number 0-7735-0076-6
Library of Congress Catalog Card Number 70-124985

Printed in Canada by John Deyell Limited

Foreword

The pieces collected here were spoken to university audiences between 1961 and 1969. They are printed substantially as given without any attempt to revise them in the light of later events or to turn speeches into essays. They record faithfully one person's reflections on varied aspects of the rapid growth and unresting change in Canadian universities in the sixties. At a time when nothing stood still, it was often difficult to see what was going on and always hard to grasp the meaning of events. I had, of course, the chance to learn from many discussions with friends and associates. Whether they succeeded in teaching me anything, they will have to say. At any rate, they helped me to uncover what I really thought.

My greatest debt for help is owed to Mr. Bernard Trotter, Executive Assistant to the Principal of Queen's University during most of this period. He was endlessly at my service in gathering material, in suggesting themes, ideas, and analogies, and in making me think again on many of the topics discussed. Without committing him to what he helped me to say, I want to thank him specially.

J. A. C.

Contents

Introduction

It was a happy editorial decision to assemble the selected addresses of J. A. Corry delivered during and after his regime as Principal of Queen's University and to make this volume Queen's first contribution to the publication list of the recently launched joint McGill-Queen's University Press. I am honoured by the invitation to contribute an introduction to this compilation, even though the author needs no introduction and his speeches speak so eloquently for themselves that an explanatory gloss is superfluous.

All the papers reproduced here were prepared for oral delivery and few editorial liberties have been taken with the texts, in order to preserve in print the informal flavour and immediacy of impact conveyed by the spoken word. The papers collectively address themselves to all the central issues that perforce become the major preoccupation of an academic called from the ranks to become the chief executive officer of his university. They demonstrate forcibly what all such senior officers quickly comprehend: analysis of the university is akin to peeling an onion, not so much from the tears it may bring in the process but simply from the involuted design that requires constant peeling to expose the core of the matter.

The varied occasions which inspired the preparation of these papers bespeak not only the dedicated, thoughtful executive officer battling vigorously to maintain the excellence of his own university; they also reveal the author's involvement and far-reaching concerns as one of Canada's leading educational figures during a seven-year period that has probably witnessed more challenge and change in higher education in Canada than the previous half-century has produced.

We begin, fittingly, with an installation address marking Dr. Corry's formal assumption of the heavy responsibility for leading Queen's University over a decisive period marked by accelerated expansion of physical facilities, student body and academic staff. With clear-headed prescience he forecasts the major issues confronting the university and announces the central themes to which he repeatedly and with ever surer grasp returns in his subsequent addresses.

In the early sixties the foremost theme was the growing reliance of universities on government financing. In a paper delivered in February 1964 we find him prophetically forecasting a scheme of provincial government financing by means of weighted student formula grants which, in fact, came into operation three years later. The way in which a busy academic administrator is obliged to allocate his time provides a ready clue to the ebb and flow of central issues confronting a university. Judging from the time Dr. Corry spent in anxious and sometimes frustrating negotiation at the provincial capital, it is fair to assume that resolution of the problem of government financing was viewed by him as the *sine qua non* for the university. It is also clear that his advice had considerable bearing on the official policy announced late in 1966 and that in the retention of this policy lies the universities' chief hope of maintaining a measure of internal autonomy for settling their own educational priorities even as they become dependent on the government for portioning out the total budget for all public goods, including higher education.

The need to develop a provincial policy with respect to operating grants for universities is illuminated, though only indirectly, by reference to his address to the annual meeting of the Association of Universities and Colleges of Canada, "Higher Education in Federal-Provincial Relations." The occasion was fraught with tension and emotion, for the federal government had just announced its intention of retiring from the field of direct support to university education through a per capita formula. It was this federal programme that in large measure had given the national association of universities its *raison d'être*. Dr. Corry, as past president of the AUCC, was called on short notice to substitute for the Secretary of State, whose public duties prevented her from coming to speak as planned. His speech, couched in typically dispassionate language and the measured resignation of a student of politics (where, if anything can happen, it will) nevertheless barely conceals the deep disappointment of a confirmed federalist. Despite the constitutional preeminence of the provinces in the field of education, it seems somewhat paradoxical, as he remarks, that the federal government would retain its concern for supporting training for run-of-the-mill tasks but opt out of the more vital educational areas. The ironical sequel to this opting-out decision is only now beginning to emerge: the federal government finds itself responsible for roughly half the universities' operating expenditures but has virtually lost control over the total size of the bill for higher education submitted to it by the provinces!

Other papers in this collection provide additional evidence of Dr. Corry's statesmanlike role extending beyond the boundaries of his own university. We find him, for example, in his capacity as chairman of the Committee of Presidents of the Universities of Ontario, addressing himself (with marked courage, considering his audience of deans of graduate faculties and heads of aspiring university departments) to the dangers of uncoordinated empire building in graduate work and to the possibly greater danger of over-playing graduate teaching and research to the detriment of the universities' long-standing concern for sound undergraduate instruction, "where broad acres are open to us all."

Again, this time in his capacity as Canadian delegate to a meeting of the executive heads of Commonwealth universities, we see him describing the emergence of faculty associations and speculating on their possible role in joining forces with university presidents to shore up the beleaguered ivory towers. Or again, this time "at liberty" as a distinguished visiting professor at McGill, he reflects aloud on the anxieties all in Academe share for the future of universities and makes a strong plea for a restoration of the splendid traditions of the great teacher in the classroom.

Finally, in recognition of this leadership and these services to higher education, he is honoured at convocations of his sister universities, and returns the honour by presenting addresses of a distinction which is not always guaranteed on such occasions. Roughly half the selections in this volume have been made from convocation addresses. They are singularly devoid of the platitudes that customarily grace such addresses, and they are remarkably unrepetitive and integrated. Their cumulative impact is impressive and instructive as every major concern of the university in contemporary society is successively incorporated into the author's frame of reference and its implications both for function and structure imaginatively assessed.

All these papers, in their literary elegance, the telling metaphor, the economy of line and amplitude of thought, tell us much about the qualities of the author. The judiciously balanced arguments bespeak the legal mind capable of incisively baring the essentials of a problem and cutting through the rhetoric and mythology that permeates so much of the contemporary discussion of the university in crisis. The philosophical presuppositions of the liberal democrat are as effectively invoked in these addresses as they were brilliantly expounded twenty-five years ago in his introductory textbook, which has had a profound influence on a generation of Canadian students of politics. In a day when the radical left finds it fashionable to dismiss the tenets of liberal democracy as irrelevant and *passé*, it is good to be reminded once again of the intellectual virtues they instil: the broad spirit of tolerance and of intellectual humility which proponents demonstrate in both thought and deed; the capacity to suspend judgement until all the arguments are in; the pragmatic willingness to compromise on means so long as the end of human dignity and potential is not sacrificed; and the incorrigible optimism despite anxieties and stresses faced by a bewildered community in the grasp of seemingly uncontrollable forces of change. These are the qualities and values that shine through these addresses: the object under scrutiny is the social institution we call a university, but the subject at the heart of the matter is the individual and the liberation of his potential as a rational being to which the university should dedicate its functions.

It is not surprising to find the author, as a senior university officer with a training in law and an academic concern for politics, grappling with the changing nature of the university, its peculiar role in and for society, and its relationship with other social institutions, particularly governments. The university as social institution is seen to be perhaps the last (not excluding the family) to be caught up in the nationalizing grasp of collectivism, forced to abandon its ivory-tower privacy and insularity as it is recognized to be an agency vested with a public interest. Governments have forced the pace of this transformation by massive infusions of public funds. With these funds comes an enlarged expectation—perhaps even an overblown one—of the services universities should be required to provide society as a *quid pro quo*. Not only does this transformation constitute a challenge to the private cultivation of learning within the traditional university, it places a large question mark over the right of the university to presume its capacity to operate as a self-governing guild. And, even as this question mark hovers over the university, the contemporary plans for internal reform of university structures envisage an enlarged role for faculty and students in the government of "their" institution. The turmoil within universities generated by the efforts to adapt to these claims for participatory rights does little to strengthen the confidence of governments and their public supporters in the capacity for, let alone the desirability of, self-government for the university.

These papers develop and illuminate the paradox of trying to meet simultaneously the equally legitimate claims of public accountability and a necessary measure of academic autonomy. The reconciliation, as the author again and again makes clear, will be neither easy nor stationary in a period of such rapid change. The precarious moving balance will require for its maintenance a concerted effort from all: conciliatory but positive leadership from academic administrators; a willingness on the part of academic staff and students to share new responsibilities (and with them some diversion from their intellectual pursuits); and a self-restraint from governments that can only be counted on if the public at large, to whose views they are responsive, can be led to an understanding of the special conditions within which the intellectual life of this unique institution must be permitted to flourish. It is the attainment of this last condition by positive efforts on the part of the university community itself that may prove to be the major challenge for the university in the seventies. As an erstwhile private institution, the university in the past could neglect its public relations more or less with impunity; today, emerging as a public institution, dependent on an understanding taxpayers' largesse and with functions that leave a marked imprint on the wider community, the university can no longer afford to adopt this egocentric posture.

Thus, in the end, Dr. Corry is prepared with reluctant realism to say farewell to the ivory tower. At the same time I would add for him a jaunty subtitle to his collected speeches: "But let us keep the aspidistras flying over the dreaming spires!" For it is to the dreaming spires that he reverts with increasing conviction. Yet, it is the hard core of the university's function, typified by the dreaming spires, which is the most difficult to "sell" to the public. The professional faculties in universities will take care of themselves: their students on the whole are well motivated, their "product" is clearly seen to be useful to society and hence good value for the tax dollars invested. It is the faculties of arts and science that are more vulnerable. Even here, however, and especially in the sciences, the intense specialization and the concentration on research have produced such obvious material benefits to society (even as they have improved our self-destructive capabilities) that there is little reason to be concerned about reluctant public support on this score. What is of concern is that these trends and preoccupations may be destroying the dreaming spires. Devotion to research has downgraded undergraduate teaching and gives rise not only to much legitimate student dissatisfaction with their programmes but also to their righteous criticism of "immoral" research attuned to the state and other large organizations capable of buying research required for their own practical ends.

While the second criticism finds Canadian universities less vulnerable than their American counterparts, the first criticism is fundamental and must be met—as so many universities are now doing—by extensive revisions of the curriculum. Nevertheless, curriculum reform by itself is not enough. What is required, as Dr. Corry so eloquently affirms, is the restoration of the status of teacher and of teaching in classroom and seminar—a return to the universities' basic concern for the instruction of our youth. Progress will be made here only if the rewards for teaching are made comparable to the rewards now available for research and graduate work. And the status of the teacher in the classroom cannot be improved "if the teacher cannot reach students where they now are," for otherwise the teacher "has no hope at all of bringing them [the students] where he now is." Prolonged exposure in our typical graduate programmes to progressively more specialized interests does little to improve the capacity of the teachers recruited from the system to relate the specialism they profess to the world about them—"to the anxieties that affect contemporary life" and form such a large part of the contemporary thoughtful students' concerns. If the dreaming spires are to be preserved we must find a balance between "in-depth" studies (including research) and the general liberal education which ideally gives the university its primary role as the developer of the critical intelligences required to operate an increasingly complex social apparatus and to prevent it from destroying essential human values.

In sum, two instructive messages emerge from a reading of these addresses—messages that should be taken to heart by all who have an abiding concern for higher education in Canada. First, in determining the status and functions of the university, all participants must recognize the need for balance in seeking to reconcile such opposing but valid goals as autonomy and accountability, research and teaching, general and specialized instruction, and education as a private affair and as a public good. Finally, and most important, we must learn, in the phrase of E. M. Forster, "to connect," to relate constantly the "means for living" to a "meaning for life." If the university fails us here it will have abandoned its dreaming spires even as it has had to bid adieu to its ivory towers.

J. E. Hodgetts

Principal's Office
Victoria College
University of Toronto

In his inaugural address as thirteenth Principal of Queen's University, 1961, Dr. Corry presents his views on education in a period of rapid social change, forecasting issues which were to assume major significance during the sixties.

The University and Social Change

When I was being asked to consider the post in which I have just been placed, I was not told, nor did I know, that the appointee would be described as the thirteenth Principal of Queen's University. Whether knowledge in time would have shaken me, I cannot say. I do know that, leaving superstition aside, there are grounds enough for apprehension. The spectre of numbers, a worry to us for a decade, has almost become a presence. The presence itself will raise thorny problems. Other, largely independent, developments must be met with careful answers. There is little prospect of cloistered calm in which to think about them. Of these hazards, I have at least been aware.

Before going on to some of these, I say gratefully that I start with great advantages. Under the Principalship of W. A. Mackintosh, Queen's University has been a happy place: there are no rooted rancours to be overcome. In this encouraging atmosphere, standards have been defended—and raised, wise appointments made, and new ventures auspiciously launched. As far as I know, we are not anywhere in untenable, exposed positions from which we have to retreat. It has become a commonplace for outsiders to say enviously, in the

1

words of Falstaff, " 'Fore God, you have here a goodly dwelling and a rich."

The greatly increased number of students soon to be begging for admission has been much talked about. The talk of numbers gives an easy quantitative measure of some aspects of our emerging problems, but it also tends to obscure more striking developments. Even without any more students at all, the most serious issues would still be there. The pressure of numbers will be an aggravation of these but not a great deal more.

Most important is the rapid thrusting of the universities into greatly enhanced responsibilities in our society. We often think we explain the new face of things by saying that the electronic and rocket revolution demands an immense increase in trained intelligence and specialized knowledge and skills. This is now a truism, which, be it noted, does not settle the question of what part the universities can appropriately play in leading the minds of the young to such knowledge and skills.

The thrusting force that pushes us is a still deeper one. The ever more rapid advance of scientific discovery and its practical application to our material concerns does more than transform the nature of occupations and professions. Along with other influences to be noted later, it is changing profoundly the nature of our society. The prospect of having to become cave-dwellers again is only the most striking impact of scientific discovery and technical innovation on our lives. In fact, every such innovation that is put to persistent and extended use has a marked effect on social relationships and the patterns of life, modifying and unsettling them in myriad ways. Countless such innovations now work upon us ceaselessly.

Along with scientific and technological advance has come the parallel growth in the size of economic and social organization, which brings huge resources of human and mechanical energy into a relatively few hands. Keeping pace at the same time has come the massing of people in cities where they are more easily served with collective facilities, more easily treated as statistical units, and more exposed to the pressures of sudden and unforeseen changes in the circumstances of their lives.

These are the main elements forcing revolutionary changes in the structure of our society. People of my age can all testify to their scope and power. The world we thought we knew and certainly were told about by our teachers has disappeared. The predominantly in-

2

dividualistic society of fifty years ago has been transformed. There is now a pronounced collectivist cast on many of its features.

For the most part, this outcome has been unwilled, unplanned, and even unforeseen in its wider and more momentous consequences. We are still far from seeing all the meaning for us of what has already happened. And the end is not yet, because the forcing agents drive on relentlessly. The result is not only a society with large collectivized segments but also one that is inherently unstable through incessant change. The power we have gained through science, technology and large-scale organization racks the society continually.

In the earlier stages, the initiative of private organizations in the economic sphere set the processes going. As the unforeseen consequences emerged, they changed social relationships in ways that were disruptive of the older customary order and aroused widespread protest. Fed by humanitarian impulse, the protest spread and deepened as the pace of change quickened and exposed ever larger groups to unmanageable situations not of their own making. Governments found themselves unable to ignore protest on this scale.

So, at the next stage, governments intervened to ease the pinches, and to work a variety of still further adjustments in established relationships in the society. Gradually, as a generation of experience with such adjustments has been assimilated, government action has taken on a wider scope and more imaginative sweep. Much of its thrust still comes from humanitarian feeling.

Whether in government or in large private organizations, corporations, trade unions, or whatever, there is now a large measure of deliberate exercise of mobilized power, with an impact upon us both wide and deep. We shall have more rather than less of it for a long time to come. The power is recognized to be there and available. Inhibitions against its use have weakened greatly. Where power is thus consciously possessed, we must reckon that it will be used.

One fairly new factor must be added. Those responsible for policy in the towering organizations of today have come to realize the power they wield and to see the often unintended consequences of its use. They have become deeply aware of the maze of human relationships that are at their mercy. Unlike professors who can suspend judgement indefinitely, they must act, and whatever they do will modify the terms of life for many and establish new social patterns for the future. They strongly want to use their power responsibly. To act responsibly, one must know the nature of the relationships to be impinged on, try to see how everything is related to everything else, and, in relation to the longer-run consequences of action, try to replace drift by mastery.

The sharply rising demand for university graduates by the highly organized sectors of our life falls into perspective. It does not arise merely from the deepening complexities of science and technology nor merely from enlarged operations and growing productivity, although these are very important factors. It comes increasingly from the need for greater foresight into the wider social consequences of the exercise of extended power. The times cry out for an imaginative grasp of the truth that everything—or almost everything—is related to everything else. There is more urgent need for systematic study of a maze of relationships that are often masked and hidden from an untutored view. Where should one look mainly for the persons with the needed qualities of mind and sensitivity?

Perhaps I overstate the degree to which this aim of greater foresight has been clearly articulated. If so, it is because I think we are likely to underestimate the forces pushing us this way. At the beginning of the modern era some 300 years ago, men in the Western World began to hope that, by taking thought, they could bring under control the terms of their existence on this planet. For a long time, we thought to do this by the way of individual freedom, making each man his own captain. More recently, as new resources and new techniques were acquired, collective action through large-scale organization, both public and private, became the more favoured method. At the same time and despite some recent pessimism, the hope has deepened into conviction. Most significantly, it has spread beyond the Western peoples to the rest of the world. Even if hopes for such mastery of the human condition are exaggerated, as I myself think they may well be, their aim does not lack nobility or grandeur. The momentum they have set going is now so great all over the world that it is not likely to be arrested except by proven failure.

All these considerations help to explain how the universities come into new positions of responsibility. A fundamental shift in the structure of our society has made it an interrelated whole which we can visualize after a fashion, and think of as a whole. We have, or think we have, the capacity in our public and private organizations to mould it nearer to the heart's desire by deliberate and calculated action. At the least, we can now change very quickly and drastically many of the conditions of life within it. The will to go on trying can be counted on because it springs from deep roots in our inherited tradition. Society will continue to be modified by purposeful action, by organized power: its present relationships and patterns cannot be taken for granted. Whether we like it or not, the persons we educate will increasingly find their sphere of work in large organizations which have powerful leverage on the social structure. So, universities cannot escape having a large responsibility for imparting the knowledge, quickening the intelligence, refining the perceptiveness and deepening the sense of personal responsibility needed to maintain our equilibrium.

Social advance and improvement, on the lines we are now working on, is to depend in large measure on purposeful intelligence, directed specifically to that end. By contrast, in the older individualistic society we are now leaving behind, social advance was to be engineered through maximizing individual freedom: it was deemed to be a by-product of the enrichment of individual lives. Society was to be improved by the interaction of numerous individuals, all attending primarily to their own affairs. Adam Smith's "invisible hand," in its providential cunning, stretched far beyond the purely economic.

For this reason, higher education has had an individualistic bias, and universities, as naturally conservative institutions, still think a good deal in the terms of that bias. Its ideal fruit was the rounded individual who could take to himself the best of the learning and culture of the past and use his quickened mind to live humanely in the present. Higher education was largely a private affair. We said knowledge was to be pursued for its own sake, meaning surely, for the cultivation the search gave the pursuer. Under individualistic assumptions, the student was allowed, and even advised, to take society for granted. Its principal relationships, generally thought to be sound and good, could be expected to stand for a long time. A few iconoclastic professors might tell him the time was out of joint, but he was almost never stirred to fear that he had been born to set it right. Oriented for individual excellence and individual achievement, he was rarely challenged by the idea that there might be a direct and intimate connection between higher education and the larger movements and arrangements of society.

Such a direct and intimate connection is begging recognition today. Even if knowledge is not being consciously pursued for the sake of power, it comes to much the same thing in the end, because knowledge is being directed to purposes that bring large social transformations, willy-nilly. The appropriate response of the universities to the new shape of things is now an issue of more fateful consequence than decisions about numbers of students. Positions must not be taken until they have been fully thought out. We must not be like the much confused but earnest woman who always had to add her piece to every serious discussion. After a particularly outrageous contribution, someone reproached her, saying, "Abigail, do you *never* think before you speak?" She retorted, "How am I to know what I think until I hear what I say!"

Nevertheless, some things can be known and said. Universities must respond to the changed structure of society in the most helpful ways open to them. Education of whatever kind is always for the service of life, and when the conditions of life change decisively, universities must adjust to meet them.

In the responses made, there must be no compromise on basic principle. The free spirit must have free rein. Universities cannot work to order or produce against a time schedule. Whatever the needs of society, the university's way to serve is always through individual excellence, freely nurtured and freely developed. Society may have become a collective organized whole capable of being grasped in thought and moulded by deliberate action. But one cannot educate societies: one can only educate individual persons.

No doubt individuals need to be aroused into new kinds of awareness and new apprehensions of responsibility to fit them for facing the radically changed conditions. In serving life in such changed conditions, however, we must not take the urgencies of today as expressing fully the needs of life. These urgencies are so great that they expose us to pressure for short-sighted policies. I have said that society is tending to become a great interlocked machine. To take as the primary aim of university education the production of efficient components for that machine would be a disaster, an abdication. So to do would almost be saying that the purpose of a university is to serve the state, a sufficient discrediting of such an aim. For both state and society, by their very nature, are trapped in immediacies which cloud the vision of the future.

If we are to have a future better than this present, if we are to master the power we now have to destroy human personality as well as to obliterate physical life, we must all become more civilized. I have not the presumption to suppose that universities alone can change the heart of man. In the civilizing process, their essential part is the enlightenment of individual minds, teaching them to see any current situation in the perspectives of time and space, and to see the patterns of relationships that show its meaning. Even if reflective thought is not the whole dignity of man, it is the element that universities can chiefly contribute to our becoming more civilized.

We need to lay bare more intellectual fibre in our teaching by attending more closely in every subject to relationships. We must attend not only to the unseen fabric that holds the subject together and makes it a teachable entity but also to the connections of the subject with the world and man. Here, too, we have something that is central to the new, enhanced responsibilities. One vice of specialization in its more extreme forms is that it often emphasizes fact-gathering at the expense of the study of relationships. The newer needs of large organizations for university graduates, whether their contours are fully perceived yet or not, are increasingly for persons who can see "the way from some thing to the whole of things," look into the opaque recesses of society and discern the maze of relationships there.

A good long step in the right direction can be taken by a simple reaffirming of essential principle. For surely the one sure test of the fitness of a subject for university instruction is that it can be made to reveal itself as a network of relations. Such subjects are the congenial stuff for the mind; it can be stretched indefinitely and its cutting edge sharpened in the persistent pursuit of relations. The imagination is stirred by seeing how much there is that hangs together. New sails are set on the old philosophic quest to know how it is that the mind knows what it knows about the world.

Any subject matter that can be explored in this way and awakens the student after this fashion is appropriate for university study. Within these limits, it doesn't much matter what a man studies as long as he can dedicate himself to it and thus release unsuspected energies and capacities. Even if, as is charged, we have been nourishing two separate cultures, the natural sciences and the humanities, they will not remain in barren isolation if each is cultivated in this way and in this spirit. The walls will be breached and the gaps bridged by people with disciplined minds sensitively alert to the wider frame in which their special studies must be set.

The issue between broad general education, on the one hand, and concentration on specialties, on the other, is to be seen in much the same way. No doubt we need more persons with a broad general education of a higher quality than ever before. Yet we gain nothing if depth is sacrificed for breadth. Only in the deep probing of a particular subject does one get pride of mastery and the correcting humility of following knowledge until it fades into mystery. More important, one cannot survey the world except from a standpoint, some thoroughly assimilated experience and knowledge from which to take one's bearings. Explorers must have a base: space travellers who spend their lives in orbit will make little of their wider survey of this planet or any other.

On the other hand, it is always wrong to teach the impressionable undergraduate to bore deeply without also taking him to the heights for a wider view. Both breadth and depth must somehow get their due. If his imagination is not aroused at this time, it probably never will be. He must learn to see the paths that lead from his more specialized interests to other fields of knowledge, learn to put the work that engrosses him into a perspective of the whole of which it is only a part. Without this wider awareness, he cannot live a full life or give his best to the specialty that finally claims him.

Indeed, I think the issue between general education and specialist education is largely outmoded in today's circumstances. It vexed us because it got its force from two opposed arguments, both derived from the earlier more individualistic views. On the one hand, there was the view that higher education was for the ornamenting and enrichment of individual lives and not much concerned with any specific social role. This was thought by many to mean that education should be broad and general. On the other hand, there was the view that society was really all right as it stood, would change little, and so could be taken for granted. This was taken, in turn, to mean that if a specialist had his specialty, that was all he needed to work creatively in a stable society. All this has been changed. Most graduates now go out to specific functions in society that call for both breadth and depth.

To go further, the issue as it has focused on the subjects fit to be taught has always been in some measure false. We all know how subjects especially appropriate for broad general education can be debased in the teaching into recondite and barren specialties contributing little to human understanding. On the other hand, to take an example, the law of the sale of goods is a technical, highly specialized subject if ever there was one. Yet, as a student, I saw it taught by a master who made it a broad general education. Economic history, changing technology, commercial practice, business organization, legal and social philosophy were all brought to bear on the relentless dissection of concrete and highly technical questions. It is not what is taught but how it is taught that matters. In very many of the disciplines we profess, breadth and depth are not closed and opposed alternatives at all.

It follows from what has been said that the narrow training of blinkered specialists is not a good enough university contribution to the needs of life in the late twentieth century. The specialist who is nothing more than a specialist will always be a servant waiting to be directed. The work of the specialist is never undertaken for its own sake but because it has its place in some larger scheme of things. Be he scientist or whatever, if he cannot move with some familiarity and assurance in this wider sphere, he will always remain a servant of purposes largely inscrutable to him and beyond his power to help to shape.

Let us have no illusion on this point. The integration of the critically important work of our society is no longer mainly in the charge of an invisible hand, guiding the spontaneous work of a multitude of individuals. More and more, integration of the work that is most momentous for us in shaping the outlines of the discernible future is in the visible hands of specific persons and committees in large organizations, public and private. Other things being equal, these posts of great responsibility will go to the persons who have the greatest capacity for grasping complex relationships, who see most clearly how the parts are, or can be, fitted to make the whole.

I said, "other things being equal." Often, of course, they will not be equal. Quite obviously, I am now talking about leadership in the broad sense. Much cant is talked on this subject, and I don't want to be taken to be adding to it. The making of leaders cannot be reduced to a formula. There are no unfailing recipes for the gaining of wisdom. These have been so far mainly the products of character and deep experience of the world. The universities will be wrong if they ever come to think of themselves as producing leaders and wise men through some programme of studies.

However, a new additional requisite for leadership and wisdom is emerging. It is an educated appreciation of the complexities of science, and of the intricate relationships of an interdependent society, which less and less will yield their secrets to character and worldly experience alone. So, the universities would be culpable as well as wrong if they failed to put their graduates in the way of being able to assume the larger responsibilities.

This is not to say that the main task of the universities is to prepare a supereducated group of persons for the control posts in a highly organized society. Thus to concentrate on higher education for a ruling élite may be an adequate aim for the Soviet Union where the leaders are confident that they know what society should be like and are willing to force human lives into the mould of that vision. We want to remain free, flexible, and experimental. It is not for us to think of producing masters rather than educated men and citizens, to think of serving large-scale organization to the neglect of the wider reaches of the community.

I have been talking, for the most part, about the emerging newer responsibilities of the universities because these are the less familiar. They are additions to, and not subtractions from, the older responsibilities. These latter, as we know, have included the education of men and women for the church, for teaching, for the older professions like law and medicine, and for entirely nonprofessional citizenship. The lives of many such persons across our country have been a prolonged instruction in civility, inducing reflection, restraint, second thoughts, personal responsibility, and community pride. From the wide scattering of such persons come many of the effective leaders of community opinion and public opinion, our defence in depth against the abuse of power, public or private.

So, if university education is to provide larger reservoirs of talent for public and private organizations, it must also feed, in greater volume than before, the scattered springs of thought and action in the wider community. If there are to be more controllers, there must also be many more persons fitted to rally opinion for controlling the controllers. A community that is to remain free and become more civilized must always have the inner capacity to impose limits on the wielders of power. The newer responsibilities give more point than ever to the older responsibilities.

I know that becoming more civilized calls for more than I have asserted. Without a vision beyond themselves, the people perish. It is widely held nowadays that we have become enslaved to the material and the immediate. The evidence for this point of view seems to me less than conclusive. I would rather say that our worst troubles come, not from the fading of vision but from an obscuring of the upward path in our immediate foreground. Nothing stays put around us any more: we lose our sense of direction in the fog of incessant change, and naturally we flounder. We can't relate what is happening all around us to the inherited values we still honour when we can't see how to move. The first charge on the universities is to throw a steadier and longer beam from the lamps of reason.

10

Contribution to a symposium at a meeting of executive heads of the universities of the Commonwealth at St. Andrews, Scotland, July 1963, summing up the role of faculty associations in the Canadian universities in the first ten years of their existence, and guessing at the future.

The Rise of University Staff Associations

The invitation to share the opening of this discussion expressed the hope that I would speak of Canadian experience and make comparisons with other Commonwealth countries. The latter limb of this hope, I should say at once, has been sawed off. The treatment is parochial, and limited to the Canadian scene. In the time available, I was not able to satisfy myself that I grasped the realities of staff associations outside Canada. It seemed better, therefore, to stick to what I knew fairly well and to leave the comparisons to be drawn out in discussion by those better placed to make them.

Although staff associations have existed in a few Canadian universities for thirty years, they were loosely organized, feebly supported, and only intermittently active until about 1950. In the late forties, university salaries, almost frozen during the war, showed little sign of catching up with the general and rapid advance in salaries and wages that had been going on for a decade. The university teachers, reflecting on this and seeing the notable improvement in incomes that other organized groups had managed to secure, began to plan a national organization for furthering their interests. The Canadian Association of University Teachers (CAUT) was founded in 1950–51. It was agreed that, in a federal country, a national association ought to be primarily a federation of locally based groups. So, coincident with the planning of CAUT, staff associations in the several universities were quickly resuscitated or formed anew. Most of them date from 1951–53.

Now virtually every Canadian university has a staff association. If formal membership is a fair index of support, Canadian university teachers take their associations seriously. Only in a few places is the membership less than half of the full-time staff. In a few universities, over ninety per cent of the staff are members in good standing. Speaking generally, membership ranges from seventy to eighty per cent, mostly accomplished in the last decade.

Although the associations, in announcing themselves, took most of the worthy, and even exalted, aims of higher education as their province, they have been active on a limited range of purposes, primarily salaries and fringe benefits, with some attention to working conditions such as teaching loads. These are the topics which fired the movement in the beginning; on these, the main weight of concern and argument have focused. This emphasis was wholly justified in the 1950s because rises in university salaries in the 1940s had failed to keep pace with the rising incomes of other groups. The staff association pressed insistently on salaries and related welfare issues. It would be wrong to say that these were the only issues in the fifties. Most associations showed a lively concern over academic freedom and security of tenure when specific threats arose. (Happily, these were rare.) Particular associations pleaded for greater library resources, pressed for reform of university senates, urged views on the siting of new buildings, arranged symposia and lectures for turning over common ground between the several faculties, and so on. But these interests were not pursued with the steadiness given to claims on salaries and staff welfare.

By 1960, in almost all Canadian universities, a very marked improvement in salaries, in pensions, and other benefits had been reached. Minimum rates of pay for the several grades of university teachers had risen by more than fifty per cent in the decade, and actual salaries for rank by substantially more than this in most places. Nevertheless, even if the salaries of university teachers have risen enough to give them the real incomes their counterparts enjoyed in the 1930s, they have not, as a group, even yet shared as fully in the greatly increased productivity as have most other groups of wage and salary workers in the past twenty years or so. So the pressure of CAUT and of particular staff associations still continues strongly on salary and fringe benefits. Whether or not refined considerations of equity would support all these demands for further sharp improvement in the relative position of university teachers, the state of the market now and for the next decade makes any such inquiry irrelevant. Competition between Canadian universities for staff, and action to repel boarding operations by American universities, make sharp rises in salaries and related benefits inevitable. In fact, salaries will rise about as fast as resources can be found, and it may be doubted how much the representation of staff associates can accelerate the process except as a distortion of the university budget and the consequent slighting of other important university purposes.

Indeed, there is not full agreement on how far the recent rises in salaries are the result of push by the staff associations. Perhaps what has happened is generally a vindication of Pareto's law on the distribution of incomes. It is proper to say, however, that the university presidents are more attracted to this view of the matter than are the staff associations.

Although, in large measure, staff associations have had trade union preoccupations, they have not used, or tried to use, the methods of collective bargaining. Salary committees of staff associations press on the presidents the case for general increases, for the raising of the minimum salaries of rank, for commitments on annual increments, and so on. They always get assurances of earnest, even prayerful, consideration, and often get, or come near to getting, specific promises of concrete action in a given year. With this they have been so far, in the main, mollified, if not content. No staff association, as far as I know, has pressed seriously to be a party to a specific collective agreement on salaries. For the most part, the associations have recognized that commitments for salary improvement cannot be separated from other items in the budget.

Recently some associations have asked for information about the amount proposed to be committed to salary improvement in a given year. The request has been refused in all instances. Perhaps this is a straw in the wind, the signal of a rising desire to share in the making of the salary schedule.

In the Canadian university, the board of governors, or board of trustees, must approve the actual budget, and the president must defend his salary and other financial proposals before the board. If he were to let the staff association share in framing the specific salary proposals, he would need to associate the officers of the staff association with his whole budget as proposed to the governors. Whether for good or ill, such action would quickly bring a revolution in university government.

So far, staff associations have had little access to boards of governors. For the most part, they have made their representations to the presidents and senior officers. Occasionally, a staff association committee meets and discusses particular problems with a committee of officers of the university. In several universities, the executive of the staff association meets with the board, or a committee of the board, to make representations about general policy but not to bargain for specific action in detail. In most universities, however, communication is between the president and the staff association. The president goes to the annual meeting of the association to outline problems, to explain policy and to be questioned on matters of worry to the association. The salary committee of the association submits requests to him and often presents them in person. Also, there is frequent informal consultation on a variety of matters between the president and the executive of the association. Presidents are readily accessible to conference, if not always open to reason. Relations range from the cordial to the tolerant, and only rarely move down the scale to the unfriendly and embittered.

Staff associations want to put the strongly held views of their members and to be assured that these will be considered. This they have achieved. In no university, as far as my knowledge goes, has there been, so far, a struggle for power as distinct from influence. This does not mean that staff associations are always satisfied with the fruits of influence. It can probably be put as an axiom of university government that the further removed one is from the actual decisions, the more one's perspective reveals what is wrong. Certainly, I myself now see less that looks like inattention, bungling and inverted priorities than I could when I was a long distance away. Everybody thinks he could quickly put some things right if he just had a chance. So it is tempting to reach for power.

More than that, university government in Canada makes little formal concession to the democratic equalitarian spirit that moves the country as a whole. Final authority rests with a lay board of governors, variously composed according to the history, character, and circumstances of the particular place. Whatever constituencies the members of the board represent, it is the exception for the teaching staff to be represented in the person of one or more of its members. The board appoints the president, holds him responsible, and insists that communication with the staff be through him. Having appointed him, normally without term, the board has to support him until its mistake in doing so approaches calamity. Almost always, the president brings a conviction of inadequacy much faster to the minds of the staff than to the board of governors. So, formal authority in the management of the financial and business affairs of Canadian universities is rather narrowly held. It is also quite closely guarded for reasons that may be good or bad, but which I shall not enter upon here.

Many members of university staffs justifiably regard themselves as being among the principal guardians of democratic values. They want to vindicate these values in their own lives and in their own work. An undefined number of them see it as betrayal for a group of intelligent men to allow control of the common enterprise they share to rest so largely in the hands of others. Many of them do not think it enough that, by law or by firm convention, control of essentially academic matters has been conceded to the senate, a body usually almost entirely made up of academics responsible to the community of scholars.

These several influences and considerations have been drawing the attention of staff associations more and more to questions of university government. Canadian university presidents are nearly unanimous in seeing a pronounced shift of interest to this issue in the last few years. The CAUT, in response to this interest, has promoted a full-scale independent study of university government, and has secured the cooperation of the Canadian Universities Foundation, fairly described as the employers' association. Some part of the membership of nearly all staff associations hope that the result of the study will be a recommendation of staff representation on boards of governors, and that such recommendation will be accepted. With salaries and fringe benefits greatly improved and their further improvement guaranteed by the conditions of the market, staff associations are looking for a larger role which will hold the interest of the membership and which will be less open to the reproach that they have a narrow trade union outlook.

If staff associations look to representation on the boards of governors, they will have to show themselves alert to the problems raised by such responsibilities. They will have to take up for study, discussion, and judgement the whole range of university policy and problems: aims and methods of university education, rates of growth as well as standards of admission, adequacy of library and equipment, as well as salaries, more effective use of physical facilities throughout the year, teaching loads as they relate to the maintaining of quality, qualifications for continuing tenures as well as for initial appointment to staff, ways of spurring laggard colleagues and moribund departments, and what not. If they think of asking to share responsibility, all these matters must come within their purview.

New circumstances now facing nearly all Canadian universities will tend to move them to ask to share in governing. Vastly greater numbers of students armed with the present qualifications for admission will be seeking places in the universities in the next few years. All universities must expand very quickly if they are to come close to providing the number of places asked for. The resources for such expansion in the private as well as the provincial universities must come mainly from governments. (Indeed, in the last twenty years the private universities have become increasingly dependent on governments.) Governments have not only acknowledged, but are now insisting that there is a vital public interest in the rapid expansion of higher education. They are increasing their grants for annual maintenance as well as for capital very sharply, but the sums needed from them will be so large that inevitably these governments will give much closer scrutiny to all aspects of university operation.

The members of the teaching staffs think they see two acute problems arising. Can the provincial governments, as they will the end of great university expansion, be counted on to will the means in sufficient volume to maintain and improve the quality of instruction? Will the provincial governments be able to restrain themselves from laying down terms and conditions that jeopardize the essential independence of the universities to teach what they think worthy to those they think qualified in the way that they think best? Already, at least one staff association in a provincial university is mustering its forces to support the president in a programme for university expansion that he is pushing upon the government of the province. Another staff association is seeking alliance with the president of its university to support him in his dealings with the government. Staff associations of the several Ontario universities are now considering whether to make concerted representations to the Government of

Ontario about the needs of the universities in these conditions of rapid expansion.

Large and rapid expansion will raise a host of issues of vital concern to university staffs in their efforts to maintain the quality of instruction. How are the numbers of additional teachers to be found and what should be the minimum qualifications for appointment? What work loads should they be saddled with? What should be the priorities in development? What standards should be required for admission to and continuance in a university? And so on. Whether the staff association in any particular university can reach and maintain a united front on these and similar issues is not free from doubt because the interests of particular faculties and departments will often diverge. Whether, in facing government in the next decade, the university will need such a united front in its staff is not entirely clear either. But it would be comforting to know that it could be counted on if needed. It must be remembered, however, that it may be difficult in certain delicate negotiations with governments to carry the staff association at the several critical stages. Staff associations are likely to plump for "open covenants openly arrived at." Some governments and perhaps a few university presidents are likely to prefer a measure of secret diplomacy. At any rate, it is very clear that in the immediate future, Canadian universities are going to be open to public scrutiny and public criticism as never before.

In the past, presidents and boards of governors have provided effective screens for scholarly seclusion in cloistered calm. The price they have extracted for this service has been the exclusion of the academics from the mundane affairs of university management. If, as I fear, they are unable to supply this service effectively in the future, they will have more trouble in continuing to exact the price.

When university policy comes under public attack, the teaching staff will want to rally to the defence. Whether their intervention would have the results they hope for is an open question, but that is beside the point. Faced with outside attack, they will want to close ranks in common cause with the president and his senior officers. If they are actively to defend rather than passively to acquiesce, they will first want university policy to be what they think defensible, and so will want a large voice, or at least fuller consultation, in its framing. Much, but by no means all, of the attention of staff associations to salaries and staff welfare in the material sense is likely to be diverted into pressure for participation in university government, or at least for more frequent consultation on many aspects of policy. How much participation and of what kinds will be wise, or even workable, I do not venture here to examine. At the minimum, staff associations will be a much larger element in the calculations of presidents and boards.

Facing public scrutiny and criticism, it is a matter of elementary caution to protect one's rear. In this posture of defence, the university needs more than ever the goodwill of the staff, whether or not it needs the good offices of a staff association. Normal line consultation with heads of departments, deans and faculty committees will not always elicit all the nuances of temper and judgement among the staff. The president and officers need other ways of reaching the staff with explanations of complex issues, of drawing on its stock of ideas and ingenuity, and of talking out matters of broad general interest. This will be particularly true in a period of rapid expansion and change compelling drastic adjustments of settled academic practice and habit. No matter how well the university management presides over the changes, there will be need for close consultation between management and the staff as a whole. The staff association provides a forum for the discussion of many issues and a way of bringing the staff generally to a focus on matters of common interest. Discussion with the staff association will, it is hoped, give the members a sense of sharing actually in the shaping of policy and will help us to reach something like a consensus on urgent matters.

Whether, in what I have just finished saying, there is any general principle for fixing the role of staff associations, I cannot say. Canadian staff associations respond to peculiar Canadian circumstances, such as the structure of university government. More than that, each association responds to the circumstances of its own community. If the president and board are effective in interpreting the sense of the staff as a whole and in meeting both problems and opportunities, the staff association will be one thing. If the university falls into tribulation, whether inescapable or invented by the president himself, it will be another thing. Close consultation with staff associations will help us to reach the first and happy consummation and to avoid the second and lamentable one.

Lecture given at Dalhousie University in February 1964, opening the case for formula financing of operating budgets in Canadian universities as a way of helping to reconcile university autonomy with large-scale governmental financing.

The University in the Modern State

In human affairs, knowledge has always been vitally important: knowledge has always been power. Wise men have always known this, and some less than wise have often had glimpses of the truth. But it is not until our day that everybody saw this light. Practically everybody knows now that the rate of economic progress, the length of our lives, the holding of our place in international competition, and so on, depend on the increase and the wider spreading of knowledge.

We are adding to knowledge far faster than ever before. We have also learned how to put it more quickly than ever to immediate use in endless ways. This makes us want more and more. We are also spreading knowledge more widely, but we are not providing enough dispensaries to satisfy the eager consumers. Universities, of course, are by far the most important finders and dispensers of knowledge. The clamour for their product brings them into public attention as never before in their history. The absent-minded professor, partially dressed in an untidy suit and wholly wrapped in his own thoughts, is no longer a figure of fun to be smiled at indulgently as the world passes him by. In a very serious sense, the world now awaits his word. The rate at which it can go somewhere in a hurry depends to a large degree on him.

However, to the great distress of the impatient who await him, he seems bemused by his own thoughts and unaware of the role he must play. The problem, it appears, is to rouse him, shout at him, push him, stick pins in him. For good reason, everyone wants to goad him on. The serious question is whether the desired results can be had in this way.

Vary the figure of speech: the university has suddenly been discovered as a goose that lays golden eggs. Everybody is excited over the promise of riches thus revealed. Unfortunately, there are unbearably long intervals between the laying of these precious eggs. Clearly, production must be stepped up. The general impatience is shared by the monarch himself, the government of the day. (In the fable, you will recall, the monarch took firm, resolute action and killed the goose so as to capture all the golden eggs at once.) Governments are unlikely to take obviously self-defeating measures. But it is possible that, in prescribing diets, jostling and reprimanding in a determination to improve fertility, they may well induce sterility.

Joking aside, the fable expresses well the dilemma faced by the provincial governments in Canada in their relations with universities. (Everything I say here about governments refers to provincial governments, because they have almost the whole constitutional responsibility for education.) Of course, the increase and the widening spread of knowledge is central to national—and provincial—growth and well-being. As many young people as can genuinely profit from things of the mind should have places in universities, to enrich their own lives as well as to strengthen their contributions to their country.

That is to say, there is a vital public interest in the improvement and expansion of higher education. To use the language of the law, the universities are now an industry affected by a public interest. Governments whose duty it is to guard the public interest would be very deeply concerned about the operation of universities, even if they did not have to provide a very large part of university needs out of public funds. If long experience with industries affected by a public interest is any guide, it points to governmental regulation and control.

Yet we know that the most precious of the gifts of the university to society can only be made by free minds with wide freedom to range. Genuinely new knowledge is hard to come by because so often it is found by persistent pursuit of what seemed to be unpromising lines of inquiry. The creative thinker has to have the courage and the support to swim against the tide, yet he is often regarded with deep scepticism by the practical-minded. The priceless element in university teaching is the liberation of the minds of students in imaginative ways that creates the thinkers and explorers for the next generations. Not all university teaching by any means is of this order. Some subjects that are taught can be taught by rote and might as well be taught outside a university altogether. Not everything a university does in its teaching and research is at issue here, but only the work that frees minds and imaginations. In our present-day society, only free universities show themselves fertile in this way. We must keep clearly in mind the delicate and complex physiology of the reproductive organs of the universities.

I must not go on to labour the obvious. It is agreed on all sides that universities must be kept free for their essential work that can only be carried on in the flexible conditions of freedom. Governments in Canada affirm this just as strongly as anyone else. Equally, it will not be denied in any responsible quarter that governments which guard the public interest and provide increasingly heavy support for universities out of public funds need assurances. How can they claim the continued confidence of the taxpayer unless they can say with knowledge that his money is being wisely spent in the public interest?

No issue of broad principle is in dispute here. The things needed are two. First, reconciliation of these principles where they come into collision, as they do when both are stated categorically without limit. We must try to define what limits can be set to the application of both while still preserving the essence of both. Second, we must devise procedures and forms of organization that will make of these principles something more than pious proclamations. The Anglo-American world knows well that carefully observed procedures are the necessary buttress to principles. Much of its genius has been in the devising of such procedures. So we should not quail before what will undoubtedly be difficult.

The autonomy a university needs for its essential job cannot be defined in a few words. The precise limits will vary with circumstances, and there will always be a grey area over which to contend. Only a few indications can be given here. A university does not need to be given the resources to teach and research into every subject that touches its fancy, but it must have the widest freedom in the way it goes about the subjects of study to which it is committed. For the teacher, this includes the right to explore and speak fearlessly, and security of tenure as he does so. For the university, working with the means available to it, its essential freedom must include the right to allocate the funds in its annual budget as it thinks best, control over its appointments to staff, standards of admission, standards in examinations and for awarding of degrees and diplomas, curriculum, and teaching loads. Secured in control of these things and assured of adequate means to work effectively up to its standards, it should be able to work out, in discussion with government, standards on intensiveness of the use of its plant and facilities, including such related issues as the length of the teaching year.

Government, assured of something like optimum use of university facilities (meaning the intensity of use consistent with maintaining the fertility of universities) and assured against unreasonable duplication of instruction and research in highly specialized fields, can give a good account of its stewardship to its taxpayers. To go further in detailed examination of operating budgets is almost certain to prejudice seriously its own vital interest in the increase and widening spread of knowledge.

Rough limits on the two essential principles can be staked out in some such way, leaving, of course, many details to be negotiated. In negotiation, universities and governments will each have to be sensitive to the other's position. Governments need to have assurances on finance, and we must all recognize that the power of the purse must be used to that end. At the same time, governments need to recognize that, for ten years at least, the greatest problem will be to get and keep enough university teachers. There is an insatiable demand for people of these abilities, not only in universities but in governments, industry and the professions. The shortage is so great that it creates a new dimension in university affairs, just as significant as the complex relationships in which universities and governments suddenly find themselves involved.

In these circumstances, it is essential that the boards of trustees and the presidents of universities are enabled to hold the sure confidence of their teaching staffs. If there is any weakening of that confidence, it will very quickly put in peril the whole enterprise of effective rapid expansion of the universities. The academic staffs will react sharply to governmental encroachment on the vital elements of university autonomy. The good teachers and the able research scholars, on whom quality depends, will not want to stay where they cannot count on promising conditions for their work. And now they need not stay. They have a freedom of choice and movement they have never had before in the history of the modern university.

If these considerations are kept in mind in negotiation, universities and governments can work to a refining and reconciling of principles, and find a pattern of viable cooperation. This brings us to the second big question: how are we to ensure that the pattern, once agreed upon, will be adhered to in practice?

Broadly speaking, I see here only one possible answer. Governments must be able to get the needed financial assurances without detailed examination and assessment of university operating budgets year by year. I leave aside the question of governmental support of capital budgets in which there will have to be some scrutiny of particular capital projects. Speaking only of annual operating budgets, there must be found a formula, or a set of formulas, for determining the annual government grants for maintenance. These formulas must be fixed so that, in the main, they apply automatically over a period of several years. I urge the device of formulas because I am satisfied that a practice of examining the proposed university operating budgets year by year will drive governments, even against their own wills and desires, into detailed intervention in university affairs.

The reason for saying so is very clear. All universities are being asked to expand substantially, if not hugely—and that very quickly. Each year then, for as far ahead as is material to consider, the operating budgets will show very large increases, away beyond the annual revenues the universities can find for themselves. Requests will go to governments to make grants to meet large prospective deficits.

University presidents are not as different from other men as they sometimes encourage people to think. (This, by the way, is a strictly impartial judgement I made of them long before I became one.) In the kind of situation I am speaking of, they face a standing temptation to indulge their worst instincts. More than that, their staffs will abet and push them to do so. Even if they resist the grosser temptations, there are always scores of things that would be well worth doing if resources could be found. I know several projects that are very good and that I am aching to try. The Queen's staff has many such that I haven't even heard of yet. Am I to reject the possibility of mounting a number of these and disappoint the staff, or am I to try it on? If there is money to be had, why don't we get our share if we can?

A government faced with requests to finance deficits in this way must examine the whole case for the grant if it is to act responsibly. It won't do just to lop off ten per cent or twenty per cent of the request of each university on a guess that more was asked than was needed. Some universities may have used restraint while others did not. To protect the taxpayer and to be fair to all the suppliants, the detail of the budgets will have to be examined. The government, or its agency for the purpose, will be driven to say, "We will support this but not that." By that very action, it imposes a judgement it is not qualified to make.

The matter will not stop there. In the nature of things, the government will often be giving the universities somewhat less than they think they need for the job in hand. And sometimes at least, the universities will be right in so thinking. Proud, vigorous universities will not readily acquiesce in what they think is inadequate support for what they are asked to do. How can they if the issue at stake seems to be the holding of their staffs? So they will resort to lobbying in the search for better terms. Surely it is wrong that government should be harassed by such importunities on policy affecting universities.

Judging each year the claim of universities to have their deficits financed will take the government deep into the whole programme of the universities. It won't happen all at once, and I am sure it won't be done by deliberate intention. It will happen bit by bit as the circumstances make one decision after another inescapable. Government will be driven steadily that way by the insidious logic of the situation.

As I said earlier, the only way I see to avoid this long-run result is to do the hard thing at once and hammer out a set of formulas which for a term of years will determine the main elements of the annual maintenance grant. It will not be easy to do, particularly where several universities of varying kinds and sizes at different stages of development are involved. Of course, it is precisely in such jurisdictions that formulas are most needed to hold a fair balance between competing claims.

A fairly simple formula providing for a fixed amount per registered student may do where only one or two universities are concerned. In the more complex situations just noted above, a double-decked device is almost certainly called for: fixed block grants of varying amounts depending on the circumstances of each university, topped off with a system of uniform grants per student.

The block grants would be designed to take account of the special situation of each university and to supplement the assured revenues of each to some equalized level where a system of uniform grants per student piled on top would cover foreseeable needs for a period of years. They would take account of the established ancillary operations which, for one good reason or another, particular universities had undertaken. They would take account of the stage of development each had reached, the approved plans for expansion of each, and of other justified peculiarities in the pattern of costs.

For the per student grants, categories of students according to the expensiveness of their education would have to be established and weighted uniform amounts assigned for each category, very high for graduate students and for medical students and dental students, moderately high for students in science and honours arts programmes, and lower for others. As registrations rose, these grants, along with fees, would provide the main flexible elements in the revenues of the universities. However, to provide against expected rises in costs of all kinds, the per student grants should rise each year by some fixed percentage.

Difficult though it would be at the beginning to fix the amounts of block grants and grants per student and to give each the proper place in the scheme, the advantages of the system in operation would be enormous. The university could calculate closely what its assured revenues for operating would be over the fixed period of years, and it could make forward plans with some confidence. It would be compelled to think about the best way to manage its affairs within these limits. It would be free to seek supplementary support from any nongovernmental source. If its friends wanted to assure it of means to give an added excellence to some parts of its programme, they could do so without fear that the government would reduce its support by a corresponding amount. With or without added funds gained by ingenious foraging, the university would have to cut its coat according to its cloth, and the vanity of dreams that beckon but are unrealizable would be dispelled.

Most important of all, it would be free within its resources to develop its priorities as it saw fit, and to carry on its programmes as it saw best. Room for variety, experiment, and full use of the exceptional advantages of particular places would be afforded. Autonomy for doing the essential job would be protected. Government would be freed from the importunities of universities and from the distasteful and frustrating job of deciding matters which the universities themselves are best equipped to decide. Both governments and universities would be in good heart for the heavy responsibilities they must face.

*Presidential address at the annual meeting of the
Association of Universities and Colleges of Canada
in Vancouver, October 1965. The universities were
having to come to grips with developments quite
outside the range of any earlier experience: headlong
expansion, massive dependence on government
financing, and an intense public interest in their doings. The Canadian Union of Students just then
was pressing for the abolition of tuition fees.*

The University and the Canadian Community

The community of which I speak is not the local community: I am not going to talk about town-gown relationships. For me here today, the community is the national community of Canada: what is the place of the university in the Canadian society?

In these days, when no nation can live unto itself, this may seem a parochial focus of interest. There is a worldwide community of scholars in which we want to affirm our membership and enlarge our part. Of course, the Canadian university has a concern for humanity that goes beyond national boundaries, but if it cannot come to effective terms with the society from which it must draw its energy and vitality, it cannot do much for humanity at large or cut much of a figure on the world stage. At this particular moment of time, our first attention must be fixed on the place of the university in the Canadian community. This is a big enough subject for me today.

The university of which I shall speak is not any particular university. When I find Queen's University as the only shining exemplar of what a university is, or should be, I shall say so expressly and hope not to be too obnoxious about it. It saves a syllable to speak in the singular and it identifies the species as having identifiable common features and problems.

Common to all and central to all is their general aim and object, derived from the models on which they rely, the universities of Europe. Their object has been the transmission to succeeding generations of the hard-won knowledge and wisdom of the past, and the discovery of new knowledge and new wisdom that will raise man's estate. It is not a mechanical transmission or a magpie accumulation of new knowledge. The aim is a civilizing mission, to liberate human minds, cultivate the imaginations and educate the sensibilities of individual human beings. Individual minds are not merely the vessels of transmission: they are the lamps that gleam and shine, and banish the dark.

I do not know of any refinements on this aim and object that are needed for our time, even though we are embarked on a period of rapidly accelerating social change which will alter the relationship of the university to the community in many ways.

To get the impact of these changes, we should recall something of the relationship of the university to the community, to which we have been accustomed in this country and which we have been taking for granted. Without attempting to do justice to the complexities of the university-community interactions over the past century, I shall look at the facets that seem to me most significant for us now.

The individualistic era covering nearly four centuries is past. But that era shaped the university-community relationships as we have known them up till yesterday, so to speak. To put it in crude politico-economic terms, the university belonged to the private sector of life: it was a matter for *private enterprise*. What the university did, what resources it had, whether it survived at all or not, was not primarily the concern of the state and governments. It was the concern of private bodies, chiefly churches and private philanthropists. I acknowledge the founding and rapid growth of many state and provincial universities in the last quarter of the nineteenth century and after. But the aim and purpose of them all remained individualistic. As in so many departments of North American life in that period, the state intervened to help individuals to help themselves.

Whether the university was provincial or private, who went to it, how their fees and expenses were met, and what they learned when they got there, were essentially private matters. At the same time, the dominant view within the university was that the purpose of higher education was the enlargement of individual opportunity and enrichment of the individual life. One went to college to better oneself;

whether that betterment was mainly material or spiritual depended on oneself. Whether it also enriched the lives of others and so contributed to community welfare also depended on the uses to which the individual graduate put his knowledge and learning. I hasten to add that, whether by design or not, most university graduates have enriched the community by their lives. By precept and example, by teaching and preaching, by staffing the learned professions, and by a leaven of rebellious social criticism, they have lifted the material and spiritual level of the community. Disciples of Adam Smith, if such are still to be found, could cite the record as an impressive illustration of the "invisible hand" at work. They could at least argue that each, by doing what seemed best to him, made the greatest contribution to the good of all.

To most members of the community, if we merely count heads, the hand has indeed been invisible. In the past, the main currents of life have not been seen to flow through the university. For most, "dreaming spires" and "ivory towers" have been somewhat derisive terms; the absent-minded impractical professor has been a figure of fun. Mature-looking people, posturing in gowns, hoods and mortarboards, like soldiers in their spurs and dress-swords, have seemed somehow incongruous, cases of arrested development, not really fitting into the serious workaday world.

As I said a moment ago, it was a matter of indifference to the public who went to university to study. There was very little interest in what the professors busied themselves with when they were not teaching. If some strange people found satisfaction in silly attempts to split the atom, preferred the dust of the archives to the dust of the arena, found the study of literature and philosophy an adequate substitute for the active life, that was their own affair. If private persons found their private lives enriched by study at a university, it was indulgently said there was no accounting for tastes. The university made relatively little impact on the workaday world.

When it did make a direct impact, the influence seemed to many to be disquieting. Young people who went to university often were shaken in their untroubled religious faith, entered a world alien to their parents and did not come back. Iconoclastic professors made attacks, deemed by many to be irresponsible, on the verities and pieties of life, leading many people to see the university as a hot-bed of radicalism, eating away at the foundations of the community rather than shoring them up.

Running through the popular mind, even if not actually dominating it, have been these currents of perplexity, suspicion, and sometimes mistrust. University people have now and then helped to intensify such feelings by contributing to images of themselves as superior beings. At the least, they have failed to practise a disarming humility. Whatever its degree, there has been tension between community and university. This becomes a matter of some importance when universities come to be heavily dependent on public support.

Of course, we have now arrived at this point. Within the last few years, we have entered on a new dimension in the relationship of the university and community. The intensifying application of technical and scientific knowledge to human affairs has made immense contributions to productivity and material welfare and has brought on a breathtaking rate of social change. Very many people see now that greater doses of knowledge can be expected to bring still greater dividends in productivity and welfare. Governments at least have grasped this truth. Knowledge is seen to be power, and gains a new respect not vouchsafed to it when it seemed only to elevate the minds and sensibilities of individuals. We must, it is said, add to the stock of existing knowledge as fast as possible and distribute it much more widely than before. Universities produce and distribute knowledge. They must be better equipped to produce more, and many more young people must go there to draw from the stock.

University propagandists have put weight behind this push by saying that the only society with any future is the educated society. In the competition of nations for power and place, the winners will be those who bet their money on higher education. Young people and their parents readily believe these assertions because opportunity opens in all directions for those with a higher education and actually closes its doors against those who lack it. Hence the unprecedented rush for university places which will not end until there are places for all who have the capacity for study at university level. It will not end even then unless care is taken to provide alternative kinds of postsecondary education which will give other keys to the doors of opportunity.

It is clear enough where we have arrived. On the one hand, it is now widely recognized that the main currents of life do flow through the university, and not around it. There is a vital public interest at stake in rapid development and adequate support of universities. On the other hand, just as these considerations are being driven home, the pathetic deficiencies of the older ways of financing universities become painfully obvious. The combination of philanthropy, religious and secular, modest government support, and students' fees will not serve any more to supply the massive capital and the up-rushing annual costs of universities. The only ready source for the bulk of the vast increases in support needed is governments.

So, in almost one breath, the university has become a public service institution, and also has fallen into basic dependence on governments for the resources it needs. Who goes there, and what is thought and taught there, have become matters of much wider public concern than ever before. I am not saying that the community generally now has this anxious concern nor that the general public demands massive support for universities from the public revenues. I do say that a much wider section of the public is now concerned, and that governments as such grasp the case for much larger financial support from them.

But what governments will do in the long run depends on what the general public will support. What that public will say when it sees how the universities are staking a claim on tax dollars that would otherwise go for highways and welfare is a matter for conjecture. Even if the taxpayer is willing to concede big expenditure on the universities, he may well say, at the same time, that the government should stop some of the nonsense he thinks goes on there. That is why it is highly relevant to consider what view the public mind has of the university.

The community and the university are now fated to much closer relationships than ever before. What will happen to the ivory towers and the dreaming spires? We can approach an answer to this question if we see clearly what has happened. The individualistic age offered a very wide freedom to universities because they were thought to be serving only the needs and aspirations of individuals. That age has ended and been succeeded by a collectivist age in which, in one department of life after another, "the invisible hand" fails to perform the work expected of it. All sorts of goals are now determined collectively instead of being left for individuals to discern and achieve. To be specific in illustration, health goals fixed by governments bring on health insurance and medicare schemes. We are now in the process of counting up how many doctors, nurses and paramedical personnel will be needed over the next decades to make these schemes effective. Collective measures will be taken to ensure that these are recruited and educated in sufficient numbers. This is only one instance of how collectively determined goals will present targets for the university to fulfil. The university, now inescapably dependent on resources supplied collectively, i.e., large government grants for capital and operating purposes, will have to come to terms.

Coming to terms does not necessarily mean governmental control of what is taught and how. A university may be obliged to educate doctors but be left—and if governments are wise will be left—free to decide what to teach them and how. But it clearly will mean governmental influence and social pressure never experienced in the individualistic age.

Speaking in the broadest terms, it is hard to find a basis for objecting to all outside influence and pressure. All the universities I know want to have a vital influence in their society. If they were to stand insulated from all social pressures, how could they know what influence is needed or will be effective? The way to have a vital role in a society is to be immersed in it, subject to its pressures, and sensitive to its deeply felt needs. Utter detachment from the hustle and bustle of one's society is a resignation from life wanted only by those who shrink from facing life. The university in the past has probably suffered from too much detachment. We can all recall instances of arid and repellent scholarship, the desperate work of parched savants who somehow got cut off from the juices of life.

Insofar as the ivory tower is a rejection of all concern with the matters that agitate the society of the day, we can say that its fate is sealed. But the ivory tower has never been an imposing structure in the twentieth-century Canadian university, and its crumbling will not of itself make any vast difference. Here its going will be a loss, there a gain, with the gains likely to exceed the losses.

The serious issues are of a different order. How severe will be the pressure of the public on the university as a public service institution? Will it be possible for the universities to insist that certain kinds of subjects are not appropriate for teaching in a university because they do not excite the imagination or stretch the mind, because they can be taught by rote and so are a waste of the talents of the highly educated university teacher? Will the university be able to retain enough freedom about the way in which it studies and teaches the subjects it must teach? To be sordid about it, will teaching loads and the burdens of various academic chores be kept down to a level that enables great teachers to go on teaching in the grand manner?

Will the teacher have time for independent study of his subject so as to ensure that he keeps alive in it? Will it be possible for penetrating and fertile minds to withdraw periodically from all the clamour of the immediate for thought and reflection on the things they themselves think worth pursuing? Will the professor's public service role permit him to persist in unpromising lines of inquiry such as the splitting of the atom was once popularly believed to be? Or other seemingly unprofitable or unpopular inquiries in literature, philosophy, history, politics, and what not?

The university teacher must be able, as part of his regular schedule, to withdraw from time to time to his study, or laboratory, to ponder undisturbed. When such withdrawal is clearly seen to be at the expense of the taxpayers, will the taxpayer be able to rid himself of the widely held notion that the professor has a soft life? The question is a serious one because, without time to reflect in an unhurried way, both teaching and research become sterile.

To sum up, we can forget about the ivory towers but must at all costs preserve the dreaming spires, which I take to be the symbol of high, unhurried, contemplative thought. If there are to be universities worthy of the name, their resources and dispositions must encourage thinking of this order. From it alone comes all the winning of genuinely new ground for the map of knowledge and the insights that make classrooms and laboratories stirring places. Without such thinking, the university becomes a factory pouring knowledge into the minds of students as they pass along the conveyor belt but destitute of any plans or designs improving the product. Actually, the university factory will be less efficient than the mass production factories we know because its product cannot be kept to a constant standard of quality. If the product doesn't get better, it is certain to get worse. Knowledge cannot be passed on effectively without inspired teaching, and inspiration dies when thought and reflection go slack.

I do not despair of preserving the dreaming spires. I see no desire on the part of our governments to control what universities do beyond the unpleasant but inescapable duty of withholding resources where they would be used for unnecessary duplicating and triplicating of facilities and offerings. (This country is not rich enough to be wasteful of the resources asked for higher education.) Our governments are pretty well aware now of how important it is for them that universities should be vigorous, imaginative, and resourceful, teaching and thinking at a very high level. If we can make it clear to them that it takes dreaming spires to do this, we have little reason to fear from governments in the way of instruction on how to do it. The big issue relating to governments still is whether, even with all the evidence now before them, they will realize how great are the resources needed to achieve the ends they desire.

Nowadays, we talk always about what governments will or will not do: we are obsessed by the importance they have suddenly assumed in our affairs. We are always in danger of forgetting that the final reckoning for the university in this age will not be with governments but with public opinion. If the public does not accept the fact that the university ranks in importance with highways and welfare, it will go on short rations. If the public mind comes to a settled conclusion that the university, as represented by its officers, teaching staff and students, is self-centred and unmindful of public responsibility, and needs to be disciplined, we had better get ready for governmental tinkering in our affairs, because votes will tell in the long run; if not with present governments, then with those that succeed them.

In many matters, it is not the hostility of the public but rather the inevitably incomplete public understanding of the complexity of the affairs and needs of the university that we ought to be concerned about. In recent weeks, when there has been widespread and gratifying discussion of university needs, everyone will have noted the heavy weighting of public attention on student aid with much less than adequate examination of other very important requirements. The particular issue of student aid is not only relatively easy to grasp. It is also related very directly to a generous ideal honoured by the Canadian community for a long time: equality of opportunity for those qualified to take advantage of the opportunities. Other aspects of university needs, such as adequate staff-student ratios, genuinely competitive salaries, the quick repairing of bad deficiencies of library and equipment, the expensive infrastructure needed for support of graduate work and research, must not be skimped.

These needs and others of the same kind are all very complex matters difficult to understand and very hard to explain to the public. I am not at all sure, for example, that I myself understand fully the infrastructure needed for graduate work and research, and many of my colleagues are sure I don't. So there is considerable risk that the public will focus on one aspect of the needs to the neglect of others that should have prior attention.

If our resources were limitless and governments boundlessly

generous, the considerations bearing on the case for free tuition would be vastly different. But we have no evidence that either of these conditions can be met in the near future. Therefore, if we are to have enough governmental support to keep the university a worth-while place for students to go, those who can themselves bear a share of the cost of their education will almost certainly have to continue to do so. It would be disastrous for the university and for the future of this country if public pressure on the issue of tuition fees led governments into establishing the wrong priorities. Student aid needs careful attention and more money, as I have said, but the current campaign for free tuition and "universal accessibility" tends to obscure the fundamental issues.

There is another consideration that must not be lost sight of. Students and parents, given substantial improvements in amounts and methods of distributing student aid, can, on their own individual initiatives, find ways of attending the university. But it is not possible for any student or any parent by himself to do anything effective at all about supplying the university with the resources it needs to make it a worthwhile place. As things now stand with us in Canada, this must be done by collective social action through governments.

It will not do for governments, under public pressure, to provide free tuition to all university students unless and until the universities have what they need to become and remain first-class institutions. Any other course, any other order of priorities, would be a hollow service in the end to the students and to the Canadian community.

We are very fortunate to be considering at the annual meeting a report of long-lasting significance for the future of higher education in Canada. Although other countries in the western world have had royal commissions or committees examining the adequacy of their systems of higher education, Canada has never had such a study because the major responsibility for education is provincial and the federal government did not have either status or responsibility to launch a study. As a consequence, the Canadian Universities Foundation, as it was then, decided to sponsor a study itself.

It reached this decision in March 1962. It took two years to find the financing and to organize the membership of the commission. We are extremely fortunate that the Ford Foundation was sufficiently impressed with our reasoning to undertake to support the study up to what turned out to be half the cost of it, $100,000. Canadian business and industry responded to our appeal to finance the residue.

I should like to express now, once more, our very warm thanks
to the Ford Foundation, and to some twenty businesses which met
the remainder of the cost. We were extremely fortunate in persuading
Vincent Bladen, Dean of Arts, University of Toronto, to chair the
Commission and were equally fortunate to have associated with him
Louis-Paul Dugal, then Dean of Science, University of Ottawa,
Senator Wallace McCutcheon, and Howard I. Ross, now Chancellor
of McGill University.

In a rapid, but searching, examination of the financing of higher
education, the Commissioners were inevitably led to analyze the
social and economic functions of higher education in Canada. Their
findings will be reviewed and commented on later in the proceedings
of this annual meeting. I think I speak for us all in saying that this is
a document of great importance to our country. We are deeply grateful, not only to those who made the study possible but in particular
to those who conducted it.

Speech made at the annual meeting of the Association of Universities and Colleges of Canada in Ottawa, November 1966. The Government of Canada in Ottawa had just announced quite unexpectedly the day before that it would no longer make direct grants to universities but would instead make additional fiscal transfers to provincial governments so that they, in turn, could enlarge their support to universities. The details of the new plan had not yet been made clear. The Hon. Judy LaMarsh, Secretary of State, was to speak at the meeting in explanation of the new policy but was prevented from coming by the pressure of public business.

Higher Education in Federal-Provincial Relations

As you know, the Honourable Judy LaMarsh was to have addressed us this evening. We all regret, and none more than I, the urgent demands of the federal-provincial conference now meeting, which deny us the pleasure of hearing her. I do not stand here to say what she would have said. Any resemblance in what I say to the message she would have given us will be purely coincidental.

Although the conference has concluded its deliberations on the question of sharing support for higher education, it is not at all clear, as I speak, what agreements will be reached and what the consequences for the universities will be. At present, it appears that any general provincial acceptance of the federal proposal will be grudging with a caveat that it is not nearly good enough. I am in no position just now to judge for myself how far the federal concessions will enable the provinces to meet the needs of both the universities and other institutions of postsecondary education. I do say it is ominous if the provincial governments continue to hold the view I understand them to be asserting just now, *viz*, that the total of the federal concessions is very inadequate.

Fully five years have passed since the universities of Canada undertook with strong encouragement, if not urgent adjuration, by governments in this country a great expansion in the provision of higher education to meet both needs and demands for this commodity. It was known on all sides at the time we undertook it that the financing of this new provision would be a very serious problem. We are now, five years later, deeply involved in the expansion, embarked on a path on which there can be no easy turning back. We are like an army launched on a strenuous campaign without having confidence that there is a reliable commissariat for ensuring it of supplies, going forward on a hand-to-mouth basis, trying to live off the countryside and on its own fat. Since the Canadian universities have never had any fat to live on, I need not say that the possibilities of improvising on their existing facilities and their own resources have come to an end. What the countryside will provide for the universities after the proposed federal supplement to its stores remains to be seen.

One thing is sure. Any further delay in putting the finances of the universities on an adequate basis will be extremely serious. If we cannot get ahead at once with new capital construction, we shall not be able to come near to doing what almost everyone in this country expects us to do. If we do not keep up in the provision of facilities, valued staff will leave us to go to jurisdictions that have solved their problems of university financing. With inadequate facilities and inadequate, low-quality teaching staff, we shall then incur the bitter resentment of thousands of young people who know that their future depends largely on the quality of education they get. They will be persuaded of what they already fear, that their elders are trifling with their lives. The most bitter reflections of youth are those that come from watching the doors of opportunity close against them. We shall lose the satisfactions of looking in a superior way on the upheaval in Berkeley. I hope these troubles are not in store for us. In the confusion of the present moment, I cannot be sure they are not.

This Association has taken what initiatives it could in trying to find answers on university financing. It inspired and organized the Bladen Commission which reported to us a little over a year ago and made a variety of concrete recommendations having to do with provincial and federal support of higher education. We reviewed those recommendations, and we sent on to the federal government, and to the provincial governments, our own recommendations based on the findings of the Commission in January of this year. The federal government, after consulting the views of the provincial governments, took interim action to relieve some of our distress by increasing its per capita operating grants from two dollars to five dollars. From that time to the present we have been waiting for a conference that is now taking place. It was scheduled to be held in Victoria in June, and with that in mind the AUCC wrote to the Prime Minister of Canada, and sent copies of the correspondence to all its member institutions and to provincial governments, to restate something of what we hoped would emerge from the conference. That conference had to be postponed and is now being held.

Whatever the outcome of the conference, the long delay in holding it and the confusion attending the discussions tempt me to some general reflections. First of all, delays in, and disappointments about, governmental action, while frustrating and paralyzing, should not surprise anyone. As soon as universities became deeply dependent on governments and therefore on political processes, we were on notice that such things can, indeed are likely to, happen.

Politics, at any given moment, is the art of the possible and not the actualizing of the ideal. In a democracy, except in times of gravest crisis, political decisions are always compromises registering the balance of forces in the society. In a continental country like ours, embracing several distinct regions and sets of aspirations, the age-old way of settling continental problems is war. War is wasteful and untidy in the extreme. We elected to try the alternative of a federal system. We should not be upset to learn that it, too, is untidy. Rather we should be grateful that it is so much less untidy than repeated wars in the settling or postponing of problems of a continental sweep.

In a working federalism like ours where both centripetal and centrifugal forces have full play, there is certain to be a good deal of dishevelled politics, temporizing, untidy and partial solutions. The denizens of universities tend to have tidy minds and to bank heavily on tidy solutions. I have almost concluded that a tidy mind is a crippling disability in dealing with the problems of the Canadian federation. At any rate, the Canadian universities are deeply entangled in the political processes I have been describing.

I do not dwell on these worrying aspects of our relationships for the purpose of urging flight from them. No escape from them is now open to us. Rather, I stress these considerations to show my sympathy for federal and provincial political leaders involved in this substitute for war. Given the variety of interests legitimately demanding consideration, perhaps the balance of forces compelled us to just this outcome. The politician is trapped and cannot look on the clash of interests with lofty disdain. Even if not actually crucified, he still has to bear the sins of the world.

So, I do not say that the proposal of the federal government for support of the universities could well have been other than it turned out to be, although I regret deeply that it got entangled with issues of technical and vocational education. Nor do I say that the provincial premiers could have done other than recoil from it. Neither do I say, although this is the hardest concession for me to make, that virtual abdication of a federal concern for higher education could have been avoided at this moment. The federal government is still engaged, nearly ten years after it lost the initiative, in a long retreat from the preeminence it had in the later years of the depression, and during war and reconstruction. Many causes contributed to this retreat, not all of them deplorable. The pendulum clearly has not yet finished its swing. The vigorous self-assertion of provincial governments is still in full spate. So it is just possible, politically, that what we have seen in the last three days had to be.

However, if I may quote Artemus Ward, "I am not a politician and all my other habits are good." Not being trapped in political processes, not being driven to register the resultant of all political pressures, I am free to say what I think. Because the pendulum must swing back and because current talk on the constitutional roles and responsibilities of federal and provincial governments in higher education is not the last word of wisdom on that subject, I venture to say what I think. In so doing, it must be made clear that I speak for myself and not as an officer of this Association. I have been careful not to consult my colleagues so they can all say that the outrage of my remarks came without warning or a chance to expostulate.

Let us look at first principles. On first principles, where should the responsibility for education rest in a federation? The answer is not easy. On the one hand, any denial, in 1867, of provincial control of education in and for the province would have made a mockery of plans for ensuring provincial autonomy. No community, then or now, can ensure its life or mould its future unless it has the say on education in that community. In any vital federal system, the province must be able to shape the main features of education in and for the province.

On the other hand, if there is indeed a nation to be spoken for and protected, then the federal government must speak for the nation, take steps to ensure its survival and nourish its growth. If the nation is also a living community, it cannot be shut out of all influence on the direction of education. At times, it may be that mere adding up of the educational effort of ten provinces will give a sum that covers federal concern in education. At other times, it will not, and then Parliament and the Government of Canada must have the power to give special emphasis and some direction to selected aspects of education. When that emphasis and direction will be needed must depend on the exigencies of particular times.

Let us look at this matter in the widest possible frame. The training of the militia, a citizen army, is a form of education. In 1867 the Fathers of Confederation did not hesitate to confer that authority on the federal Parliament because a sturdy, trained militia might well be vital to the security of the nation. Today, when a sturdy militia, whether well trained or not, seems largely irrelevant, other forms of much more sophisticated skill are vital to the nation. At any rate, the arguments of the Economic Council of Canada are fully convincing to me and I shall not rehearse them here. In the competition of nations for power, place and welfare, the prizes are going to the countries that bet on education. Can the body responsible for the peace, order and good government of Canada blandly assume that ten provincial governments, each thinking for itself and about its own needs, will produce all the highly educated skills that are needed? The Government of Canada, on mandates given to Parliament by the people of Canada, undertakes a wide range of complex functions, many of which call for civil servants with a great variety of skills. Does the Government of Canada do its duty if it fails to make sure that enough people acquire these skills?

In a number of quarters, we are being warned that the very existence of our country depends on vastly more Canadians becoming bilingual—in essence, acquiring some facility in French as well as English. Without judging this contention but allowing that it may well be so, could we count on nine English-speaking provinces grasping this urgency and making the necessary educational provision? Would the sum of these efforts add up to enough? Is it not clear that there may well be the need for emphasis, support, and direction provided by the Government of Canada? Is it not strange that numbers of those who warn us of the critical nature of bilingual needs should in almost the same breath be saying that the Government of Canada has no role to play in education?

But, it will be asked, does not section 93 of the British North America Act give exclusive power over education to the provinces? This is correct, subject to a limitation that is likely to become more portentous as time goes on. Literally, the words of Section 93 are "In and for each province, the Legislature may exclusively make laws in relation to education." If there are national needs and objectives that require concerted educational policy in two, several, or all provinces, no provincial legislature is by itself competent in the matter, and judicial interpretation on other comparable aspects of the distribution of powers under the British North America Act makes it clear that Parliament is competent, under the "peace, order and good government" clause.

It must be on this ground that Prime Minister Pearson, in his proposal to the federal-provincial conference now meeting, asserted federal jurisdiction in the training and retraining of adults for participation in the labour force. It is to be hoped that a reading of this particular assertion along with other general disclaimers in the text of his proposal about federal authority in education will not give rise to inferences that the federal government has neither status nor lively concern in the education of highly skilled and highly educated manpower in the universities. It would be incongruous to be asserting federal authority over training for run-of-the-mill jobs in the labour force and abandoning it totally for all professional, scientific, and technical personnel educated by the universities. It is the latter who will be critical for national objectives in the future.

At a time when the federal government is attempting to make clear that it has a constitutional responsibility for adult retraining programmes, for research, and for cultural development, and that these are not, constitutionally speaking, educational matters falling within the jurisdiction of the provinces, from which the federal authority is excluded, I think it timely to recall that in 1867 none of the newly formed provinces regarded university and college education as being a matter for provincial jurisdiction. All the universities then existing (including my own) operated under royal charters or other non-provincial authority. Since then provincially supported institutions have developed, but these were not considered to be the exclusive responsibility of the provinces. Indeed it is worth noting that McGill University and Queen's University, to name only two, were in the habit of appealing from time to time to business, industry and individual benefactors on the grounds that they were private institutions catering to a national (and in some respects international) constituency.

It is only within very recent years, since the provinces have provided immensely increased support for universities, that they have become concerned to exercise substantially increased control. To the best of my knowledge no province has yet claimed exclusive jurisdictional control. Universities and colleges are free to solicit funds from business, industry, foundations and benefactors inside and outside Canada. Most provinces in addition are prepared to accept a federal concern, and the federal government should be reluctant to disclaim its concern.

The federal government has constitutional ways open to it to secure the educational objectives that are vital to the nation as a nation. The number and importance of these are bound to increase in the future. One important means to secure these is the power of the federal Parliament to dispose of its tax revenues as it sees fit. So grants to students by way of loan, bursary or scholarship are within its power as also are grants to individuals for the conduct of research. It seems to me very important for the national welfare to understand that federal initiatives of this order are clearly constitutional. The only problems that arise in using them are political. And of course, as I suggested earlier, these may be formidable enough to make a politician fear to tread where a professor would rush blindly in.

Having spent most of my allotted time in strictures on the politicians and their improvisations, I want to finish in pleasanter and more cheerful vein in which I am sure we can all join. While governments have not yet solved our urgent problems, we all have great satisfaction at, and take encouragement from, the deep concern shown by all the governments of Canada over all forms of postsecondary education. The bias of the academic mind is to study long before acting. I know governments cannot always do that, but I am far from sure that the needed and likely forms of postsecondary education, other than universities, have been fairly explored, let alone thoroughly surveyed. I strongly hope that careful studies of these will proceed and that the arrangements about to be entered into now by the governments will not be regarded as permanent until these studies have revealed fully the dimensions of the problems facing the universities, on the one hand, and the remaining forms of postsecondary education, on the other.

Convocation address at the University of Manitoba in May 1967. In the previous year, there had been student sit-ins, strikes, and attendant disruption at the University of California at Berkeley and at the London School of Economics. Vigorous protest by small groups of students had come at several Canadian universities. It was clear that the postwar quietude and seeming apathy of students on Canadian campuses were over.

The University and Student Initiative

I should like to congratulate you, the members of the graduating class this morning, on having cleared all the hurdles and eluded all the traps set for you by your teachers, on having staggered across the finishing line, breathless, I am sure, and some of you perhaps even a little incredulous. Some of you may be puzzled about how you arrived here, and I could not undertake to relieve your perplexity. Some minor miracles there may have been. I do know, however, that this University is jealous of its stamp, rightly determined to protect its enviable reputation. It does not set its seal on your efforts lightly. So you can be sure that you possess some combination of ability, application and persistence, good reason for holding your heads high.

Today, you not only take the degree you have earned: you enter into full membership of this University community. I know that those responsible for its welfare will want you to take your membership seriously, because it, and other Canadian universities, need the interest and loyalty of alumni as never before.

I want to emphasize this. One American university, not to be named here, has been described as being under siege. No Canadian university, as far as I know, is thus invested, but most of them are under reconnaissance by forces not yet clearly identified as friendly.

All Canadian universities are heavily dependent on governments for financial support, and so subject to critical examination from that quarter. The taxpayer is finding the burden of university support a grievous one. He is ready, if not eager, to criticize in the hope that the burden can be reduced. The public does not readily see the university as a bastion protecting territory on its behalf. So from time to time, reconnoitering parties, howling like dervishes, circle the academic tower, loosing bolts in its general direction. The universities need friends in the surrounding territory, interpreting their role in society and ready to share in their defence against misguided attack. The graduates of the universities are called to this service.

Although not under siege from without, the garrison within is under stress and strain. For the past six years, the universities of Canada have been growing in enrolment, physical size, and diversity of offerings at an extraordinarily rapid rate. They are being transformed, their essential character modified willy-nilly, and often without the full assent of those who work in them.

At best, rapid growth and drastic change cannot be altogether orderly, even when managed well by intelligent people. Most of us get shaken up by having suddenly to do things differently, and being pushed, as a consequence, to adjust well-worn habits of thought and action. When the gap between the new ways of doing things and the habits of thought of the doers widens too rapidly, we get signs of stress. Add to this the fact that very many university teachers have had to be drawn into the planning and development of the new scale of operations. Few of us can give full and proper attention to what we are doing this year because of the distractions of what we must be ready to do next year. We suffer from the stress inevitably produced by rapid change.

The remarkable thing is that we have managed such rapid change and adjustment without any open signs of genuine disaffection in the garrison. There is, it is true, some disaffection in the student ranks, but the disaffected group is, in most places, tiny. Even within the small alienated minority, many of the seeds of disaffection were planted and nourished into growth long before these students reached the university by fundamental and rapid change in society at large.

I do not deny for a moment that the last few years have been a trying time for university students. If you have not found it trying here, you must count yourselves as highly favoured indeed. The distractions of rapid growth have interfered somewhat with the attention the student reasonably expects from his teacher. The student, like everyone else, needs, even if he sometimes does not want, firm and fixed points of reference by which to order his affairs. But nearly everything is in flux. Stability is lacking in the university world.

In fact, the flux and instability are not confined to university campuses. Under the pressure of fantastic new technology, sharply rising populations, and greatly increased economic surpluses available to commit to new adventures like flying to the moon, our society is changing very rapidly and at a steadily accelerating pace, with no slowdown in sight. Indeed, I do not think that the restlessness so evident among students today is primarily caused either by what the university does to them or fails to do for them. It is not the uproar on the campus, the beat of the hammers, the scream of the saws, the distraction of their teachers by the need to plan for next year, and so on. Without arguing at all that we are doing well enough by them, I am satisfied that, with the ampler resources now at our call, we are teaching what we teach more effectively than at any time in the past. The main root of the distress is the severe shaking up of the society in which we live.

Granting that there is to be a world, that we are not going to blow it up, the student does not know at all what kind of world it will be, except that it will not be his father's world. He does not know whether it will give him a fair chance at meaningful work, or how far the ideals and standards by which we have given meaning to our work and our lives in the historic past are a good enough response to the conditions of life he will face in the future. How could he know, when the future is unpredictable as never before in our memory. He does know the time is out of joint, and even more alarming, he knows that his elders don't know how to put it right. So, as the young have always done, they blame their elders for making a mess of things. No doubt we have failed to a degree, as all earlier generations have failed. Our humility in the face of the sad knowledge that we cannot always mould the world to our heart's desire is interpreted as passivity or complacency. So, it is held, you can't trust anyone over thirty. My own cynicism is of a grander order and extends to those under thirty as well. To quote a highly reputable source, a former Vice-Chancellor of Cambridge, "We are none of us infallible, not even the youngest."

Of those over thirty who can't be trusted, a goodly number are outraged by the demeanour of the small minority of students who kick over the traces. Influenced by press reports to exaggerate the scale of the baulky behaviour and unaware of the new stresses that feed student fear and anxiety, they complain of base ingratitude by students who "never had it so good" as they clearly have it now. (Because these critics include many taxpayers as well as professors, universities clearly have to worry about damage to their public image and public support.) Anyway, many of the older people I am talking about will want to cheer the outburst of the college professor in the United States who said: "Indulged, petted, and uncontrolled at home, allowed to trample upon all laws, human and divine, at school, the student comes to college. But too often he comes with an undisciplined mind, and an uncultivated heart, yet with exalted ideas of personal dignity, and a scowling contempt for lawful authority and wholesome restraint."

The professor said this in 1855, scoring a point for those who say there is nothing new under the sun. But I am insisting there is something new here, more than the age-old tension between old and young: in fact, the ceaseless pulverizing of our social structure by profound social change.

The most hopeful sign in this situation is that students more and more refuse to take all this lying down. They have become alert to issues in the world outside the university and are determined to say their say about these as well as on domestic affairs within the university. Only yesterday, so to speak, students' apathy and indifference were being deplored. Quite suddenly, about four years ago (before Berkeley, I want to insist) there was a change. No longer is it thought nobler in the mind to suffer the slings and arrows of an unmanageable world. Instead, one takes arms against a sea of troubles, enlists in a cause, fights back. Where so much around us is unstable and shifting, the certainty of a commitment, however ephemeral, is *something*. Some of the commitments students make are short-lived, and also, to me, injudiciously chosen but not to be scorned on that account. Commitment with passion is miles ahead of neutrality and indifference.

One of the commitments of students that is laudable and seems likely to be enduring is the determination to improve the university for those who will follow them. Students today are claiming a larger share in the running of universities than at any time since the Middle Ages. Like Aristide Briand, who thought war was too serious a business to be left to generals, many students now think university

48

education is too serious a matter to be left to professors. To a degree, they are right. Universities in which the scholars and teachers have been entirely a law unto themselves have usually gone to seed. I am quick to add that nothing in our present situation exposes us to the risks of that kind of autonomy!

Responsible and serious student involvement in discussion of many aspects of educational policy is most important. In every university, there are many committees and subcommittees where the substance of academic policy is hammered out. Students can properly seek representation on such bodies, where, aside from the constructive help they can give, they will learn why so many things are so often as they are. Hoping that this knowledge will not be too disillusioning, I add that student representation on senates and boards of governors is a different issue and a marginal one. In any well-ordered university, these bodies are rubber stamps for nearly all decisions except those of high policy. Issues of high policy of a difficult nature that involve extended debate and close decisions on voting call for long experience and judgement based on that experience. On such matters, in the nature of things, students have little to contribute.

I know that being closeted with the kings—in this instance, the senate and board of governors—is always pleasant to contemplate. In realization, it is nearly always disappointing to find out that the real decisions are made by "the mayors of the palace" behind the scenes—in this instance, the committees and subcommittees I have just mentioned.

Much of the student commitment is commitment with passion. Even this is not to be deplored since little is accomplished without a degree of passion. But passion is destructive except as it supplies drive to disciplined minds. There is a danger that passionate commitment will be incompatible with the detachment we should bring to our thinking and studying.

The chief service of universities to society and their chief glory is not the piling up of useful knowledge to support the material side of our lives. It is rather the protecting and nourishing of the traditions of civility on which all civilization in the end depends. University education should be, above all, a training in civility. And this requires us always to get at the facts, to look them in the face, to look at all sides of the question, to credit those who oppose us with goodwill and some glimmer of good sense until the contrary is proved. It requires us to give our minds as well as our feelings to the issues of life that are often clouded with contention and rancour.

Commitment to improvement of the university is not a student monopoly. Others are working at it too, and commitment must be compatible with detached and civilized discussion about ways and means. A university fails sadly if it cannot bring to bear on its own affairs the methods of thought, tools of analysis, modes of reflection, and conventions of debate that should be central to its teaching objectives.

In short, we must have civil and rational discourse. So, I find distressing the tendency among some of those pressing for a more effective student voice in university affairs to overlook this vital requirement. Some of them seem to me so determined to win their point right away that they are unwilling to listen to any other side of the story, and ready to use, if they can, the strong-arm methods of political pressure. Moreover, slogans like "participatory democracy" and "open decision-making" are repeated as if they provided millennial solutions for everything that ails us. At the same time, there is an unwillingness to define these slogans with enough precision for us to be sure we are all talking about the same thing.

As long as the talk is loose and imprecise and as long as universities are being threatened with outside influence on their internal dispositions, student initiatives will be hampered rather than expedited. Nothing will be gained by dividing the university community into adversary groups and turning it into a microcosm of the politics of Manitoba, or Ontario, or Canada.

A university community is not a society like Manitoba or Canada with a welter of contending groups and conflicting purposes that have somehow to be compromised and reconciled, often by dubious methods, if we are to live together in peace. The ends a university should be pursuing are not a matter for pitched battle among diverse groups with sharply opposed interests inside the university community. The university has work to do and we all know pretty well what it is. The means by which these ends are to be pursued and priorities among them determined can only be settled by rational discussion and persuasion. No other way is open to the university community whose mission it is to be the chief custodian among us of the tradition of civility.

Of course, custody of this tradition makes demands on others besides students. Boards of governors, senates, and university teachers must give careful attention to the more thoughtful and mature student initiative. The students of today will not respect the university unless they see high standards of civility observed in the conduct of university business, and themselves recognized as junior members of the community. The proper role and place of the student stands high on the agenda of university business. That role and place will have to be redefined by discussion in the light of changing circumstances and aspirations. Because student leaders seem likely to press for too much too fast and university teachers and officers to be rather too strongly committed to the customary ways, mediation will be needed in the process of redefinition. What better prospective mediators are there than recent graduates who understand and sympathize with student concern but whose commitment is no longer to a particular constituency but to the welfare of the university as a whole? This is the charge I put on you today.

Address given at a Convocation held in 1967 at Queen's University to mark the 125th anniversary of the opening of classes there. A university which, for more than a hundred years, had been a wholly private institution had very quickly become, in the preceding decade, a public university for all practical purposes. Heavily dependent on governments for operating revenues, and facing new public responsibilities as a consequence, it had to begin rethinking its position and priorities.*

University Education:
Prospect and Priorities

To talk about university education, one has to declare oneself on its purposes. But the aims of university education have been so much conned and recited that it is hard now to lift talk about them out of stale ritual or vacuous cliché. How does one say anything fresh about them?

The aims are many: the passing on of our inherited exact knowledge, the pursuit of new knowledge at the frontiers, the sharpening of intellects and the disciplining of minds to respect both facts and logic, the recruiting of new friends of truth, the opening of eyes to beauty in all its forms, including the elegant architecture of a reasoned demonstration. All this to lead on to understanding and compassion for the restless reaching of the human spirit for the superlative in some form or other in a world that does not easily yield such prizes. And still further on to the refining of knowledge and judgement and sensitivity into the beginnings of wisdom about "the troubles of our proud and angry dust."

All these aims have had their claims extolled before. I shall not ring the changes on them here. They are listed only to remind us of the range of entirely proper objectives a university may take, and of the large resources it needs if it is going to work at them all in high style, challenging and stretching the minds of the best students. It

**Published in Queen's Quarterly, LXXIV, No. 4 (Winter 1967).*

does not follow, however, that entrance to university should be limited to the "best" students, in this sense. Not even the greatest universities in their greatest periods have been able to do all this for all their students. Students can be led to these fountains of knowledge and insight but they cannot be made to drink equally of all the waters. We need not regret this as long as students of moderate thirst do not absorb so much of the available energy and resources that they set the essential tone and measure of all the university's work.

Of course, it is vital that students who want to explore the heights and depths can, given passion and initiative, do so effectively. However, even among the ablest and even with the inspiration of gifted teachers, the numbers of the explorers of the outer limits are likely to be relatively few. For them, the opportunity is enough, but it must be there.

The fact that many students have, and will have, strongly utilitarian interests is all to the good as long as their numbers do not overwhelm us and their interests do not dominate us. The world's work must be done. Much of that work requires knowledge and disciplined minds of an order that universities are best equipped to provide. The universities need to keep in close touch with the workaday world. Common sense and practicality never come amiss, even in universities. Again, however, it is essential that the temptation and opportunity to reach beyond utilitarian interests should be open before them.

Such opportunity is all the more important nowadays when the charm of predominantly utilitarian interests is diminishing for many students. The rapid rate of social change with its consequent unrest, the haunting fears of thermonuclear holocaust, the crumbling of older verities and certainties, all cloud the future and stir the student into anxious questioning of the whole human enterprise. There is now a concern about the nature and destiny of man far deeper than anything hitherto known in my lifetime. You have only to listen to the talk of students today to know that. There is a rapidly growing demand for education in breadth that bears directly on the apprehensions and questioning in their minds. It comes from students too concerned about the state of the world, and too eager for action in it, to be tempted into the detached scholarship that attracts the few. Satisfying this demand requires universities to have rich and varied fare to offer.

Yet it remains true that the university does not have to realize, in the education of every student, all its legitimate aims and objectives. This would be utopian. What it has to do is to hold ready for its students opportunities for study in depth and breadth, knowing that individual students will choose variously with varied results. This has its advantages because with scarce resources (and in a university, resources are by definition scarce) there are limits to what can be done. The university cannot put all its hardware into this capability to the neglect of other duties.

Indeed, universities collectively, as well as individually, will have to settle on priorities over the whole range of legitimate aims and objectives. Every individual or organization that wants to act rationally must do this because life never makes it possible to do all we aspire to do. In part, this can be achieved in higher education by division of labour, sometimes between the universities of Canada as a whole, but more often between the universities of particular provincial systems. The main areas for division are graduate work and research, where forbidding costs make division imperative, despite the forbidding difficulties. But priorities, or at least varying emphases that may shift from time to time, have to be set, within any given university, between graduate and undergraduate work, between research and teaching, and in the relative weight to be given to undergraduate offerings and instruction in different faculties and departments.

This sorting out of priorities and emphases is the most difficult and the most urgent issue facing Canadian universities. It is difficult because our past circumstances never permitted us much choice, and so denied us practice in making choices. It is urgent now because of drastic changes in the circumstances of the universities in these last years. First, the rising demand for access to university education has made a much larger section of the public deeply interested in the universities. Second, the urgent need for vastly more highly skilled, extensively educated people has made other sections of the public keenly aware that the welfare of society as a whole is heavily dependent on what the universities do and how they do it. Third, governments, which are the instruments of society for seeing that society's most urgent needs are met, have become the principal source of university revenues. Universities are so heavily dependent on governments that, for all practical purposes, the dependence is complete, giving governments enormous leverage on the universities if they choose to use it. The extent to which they do use it will depend on the temper of public opinion to which in the long run, governments must respond.

The universities will not be able to fend off an interventionist public opinion merely by pointing to the long standing custom of *laissez-faire*, which has allowed them to teach and study what they themselves like in whatever ways seem to them best. The public is now the leading patron of nearly all university activities. Throughout history clients have often found patrons unpredictable. Artists dependent on patronage who have nevertheless managed to remain true to their art have had to study their patrons as carefully as they studied their art.

For the sake of stark clarity, I have put the matter too crudely. The universities have an obligation to society as well as to the arts and sciences they profess, because society needs many services they alone can provide. So there is a duty to think hard about the priorities needed to redeem this obligation.

To those who cling to the classical conception of university autonomy, this may sound like rank heresy or craven jitters. It is neither. In their original foundations, all, or nearly all, universities were set up to serve what were thought, in a broad sense, to be important social needs. Queen's University was established to minister to the needs of a Presbyterian community for spiritual guidance and consolation—and who will deny the need? Universities have been at their vital best when they were interpreting the felt needs of society in a discerning way. They have been at their worst and their most sterile when they have neglected their trust and lost touch with the urgencies of their society. Universities in which scholars and teachers have been entirely a law unto themselves over a long period have usually gone to seed. Episodes in the history of renowned universities certify to that.

Of course, it is also true that universities have been at their second worst when badgered, intimidated and directed by clamorous agencies or towering authorities external to themselves. Like all bodies whose service it is to seek truth, they need freedom to do their work in their own way. Honest and perceptive scholarship, imaginative research, and inspired teaching—and these are what society really needs—can only be elicited in a climate of freedom. Honest and independent-minded men and women—and only such are suitable for university duties—will not work in cages, and they will not stay in institutions that seem to them like cages. If they do stay, it is because they have ceased to be that kind of person.

56

It will be said, of course, that the public ought not to be asked to pay professors to indulge their passion for useless knowledge. Aside from the awesome problem of deciding, in any long perspective of human needs and interests, what knowledge is useless, the answer is that a price always has to be paid for the gains of individual freedom. Even if society has to support some scholarship whose utility is gravely suspect, it is a small price to pay for holding free-ranging and eager minds to the service of the universities and of society.

Of the services that society needs from genuinely free universities, the most delicate and difficult, in the new environment I have spoken of, is the function of social critic. Every organized society remains imperfect, and so needs systematic examination of the substance and the mechanics of the just and unjust. The free farmer of the nineteenth century could readily diagnose and prescribe for the ills of his simple community, and he felt utterly free to criticize. The urban industrial society of today is terrifyingly complex. Its pathology is a distinct province of knowledge, and prescriptions for cure and care have to be sophisticated. More than that, those who are enmeshed in the webs of the massive organizations that dominate it are inhibited from drastic criticism. For the most part, the vital critical role must be carried by highly informed persons who are not themselves organization men.

It is not suggested that universities should take the whole burden of this role. Rather, they should be keeping at social analysis and diagnosis, awakening the critical faculties of their students, arming them with knowledge and techniques, to the end that their graduates, dispersed through society, will be leaders in keeping the *status quo* under review. Of course, university teachers and scholars must be free to take part in critical examination of our social arrangements, and we shall be the worse for their failure to do so.

As already urged, this is a delicate and difficult role to be called on to play. Interests that feel themselves threatened by the pattern of teaching carried on in universities, and by strictures issuing from university people, will object to public funds (taxpayers' money) being used for such purposes. They will say that we bite the hand that feeds us, and urge that the universities be put on a tight leash until this propensity has been subdued, and university people become "boosters" rather than reformers.

There is a further dimension to the delicacy and the difficulty. Unless and until we develop some other large-scale arrangements for providing the scientific expertise and educated skills that society in this age must have, universities are the main source of that provision. The universities may be dependent on the state, but the great collective organizations of our day, including governments, are dependent on the universities. More than at any other time in history, knowledge is power, and to be the main provider of knowledge is to have the means to great power. As nearly always happens, those who have the keys to power will use them. So, universities come to share temporal power. Without being presumptuous enough to say the universities are, or have been, bearers of spiritual power, the analogy between the universities and the mediaeval church becomes a tempting one.

The universities are a source of wonder and mystery that passes normal understanding. The laboratories, computers, and libraries excite somewhat the same kind of awe as did the rituals, liturgy, vestments, and stained glass windows of the mediaeval cathedrals. While university students and teachers certainly do not claim benefit of clergy, the universities themselves are exempt from taxation! Members of university staffs sometimes sound superior, unwittingly no doubt, when they make bold to criticize the temporalities that occupy the ground around them. In this, they suggest an analogy to the troublesome priests who were such a vexation to mediaeval rulers. While resisting stoutly the temptation of this analogy, I still see no escape from continuing tensions between universities and the governments that support them. Tension is fruitful, indeed indispensable, to the vigour of a society as long as it is kept within bounds, but within bounds it must be kept.

So, while defending their internal freedom on the broadest grounds of social policy, universities should be thinking always how to be both loyal and responsible servants of society and a fountainhead of responsible and informed criticism. Self-discipline is the most hopeful defence against discipline from the outside. This brings us back to the need for sorting out priorities. Within all the legitimate aims and objectives of universities talked about at the beginning, which should we now be stressing most? Where should we be increasing our emphasis and, if we haven't enough resources for everything, where should we lighten the emphasis, where mark time, where cut back the commitment?

Seeing that the call is for examination and thorough discussion, this is not the place, even if there were time, to be prescribing. All I shall do is suggest some areas for examination where our decisions will have a bearing both on meeting our direct obligations to society and on our retention of freedom to perform them.

Most Canadian universities are in the early stages of development of postgraduate studies in a wide range of subjects. This is a much-applauded departure because all keen teachers like to have disciples who raise the excitement of exploring the further reaches of a subject. The postgraduate student is a better prospect for the purpose than the downy-cheeked undergraduate. Good teachers know, too, that to remain good they must keep alive in their subjects, and lively research interests help to that end. All this is for the better.

However, the excitement of these new ventures and the claims they make on energies have come at an awkward time. They have come along with rapidly rising undergraduate enrolment, large classes, and a shortage of tried and tested teachers. As a result, the quality of undergraduate teaching is exposed to some peril by the competitive presence of postgraduate students. The universities themselves share responsibility for tendencies in this direction. They have not always made it clear that devoted and skilful teaching of undergraduates is as good a passport to promotion and other recognitions as are achievements associated with graduate work and research. Perhaps they have been expecting more, in both undergraduate and graduate teaching, than the available corps of teachers can give, and it is thus again a matter of clarifying priorities.

We have to consider seriously how good postgraduate work is going to be if undergraduate studies are not carried at a high level. Clearly, some of the research and some of the advanced specialized training needed can be provided in research institutes and other agencies outside the universities. Only the universities, and no one else, are going to provide systematic and liberal education for undergraduates. If they do not do it, it will not be done.

Moreover, much the largest part of our duty to society is in undergraduate education. The great mass of students are, and will be, undergraduates. The quality of attention and education they get will pretty nearly determine—and rightly so—the judgement of the public upon us—something worth remembering.

In most universities, the majority of undergraduates are, and will be, in the Faculty of Arts and Science. A big part of our obligation is focused here. It is also the area where universities have the greatest freedom to set their own patterns. In the professional faculties and schools, professional standards determine a large part of the curriculum and leave less freedom to set the measure of the education. So I shall say here only that, in setting priorities in the general university budget, support for professional education must take account of the heavy obligations to general education.

Aside altogether from such questions, it is necessary to consider priorities and emphases within the Faculty of Arts and Science. Many subjects of study which, in the nineteenth century and earlier, were covered by the cloak of Natural Philosophy have emerged as independent disciplines, highly complex specialties, often spawning numerous subspecialties. (These are, of course, what we now know as the natural sciences.) Moreover, the great prestige of the natural sciences and scientific method has moved the studies that have to do with man and the way he fits into his world strongly in the same direction. In the several fields of the liberal arts, specialties and subspecialties also flourish.

In many circles now, a higher respect is accorded to the man who digs deeply in a sector of almost any field than to the one who commits himself to trying to get a rounded, general view. This pushes many scholars into deeper and narrower specialization, and the excitement of pioneer discovery in the depths of a specialty weakens for many the attempt to see the entire human enterprise, and to see it whole.

Very strong pressure in this direction has developed suddenly and recently with the big upsurge in postgraduate studies. The graduate student is not bent on broadening and deepening his general education. He is immersed in specialized studies. He comes out with a graduate degree and a very heavy investment in a specialty on which he hopes to realize annual dividends in his life work.

All this is easily understandable and anyone who complains about it takes on a heavy burden of justification. Specialization is the price to be paid for the rapid winning of new knowledge. The accumulated knowledge that lies around us everywhere is so vast that a rounded general view which takes proper account of what is known is nearly impossible. The rate at which new knowledge is being gathered makes the enterprise still more forbidding. The man who aspires to the rounded and general view and spreads himself over a wide field exposes himself to the comment that if he only knew a little about the subject he is talking about at the moment, he would know a little about everything!

Yet it is important to consider some consequences of heavy specialization. The man who becomes an erudite specialist to the neglect of other subjects that touch on his own, and at the cost of denying himself experience of other dimensions of life, does not know at all how his knowledge, be it ever so profound, fits into the scheme of things entire. Even specialists in the liberal arts, who want to be objective after the fashion of science, are tempted to confine themselves to problems that are measureable by scientific standards. Insofar as they yield to this temptation, they exclude from their consideration the aspiring and evaluative side of man's nature, a dimension that must have an important place in a general, liberal education. If we can't talk about what constitutes the good life, is there much point in talking at all? Yet the tendency about which I am speaking is strong enough to have provoked this comment: "The sort of prudery that once proscribed the discussion of vice now proscribes the discussion of virtue."

Narrow specialists of whatever kind are ill fitted to share in determining the uses to which our vast new scientific knowledge is going to be put in our social life. But we know it will continue to be put to use there, adding new factors of complexity to our society and forcing a still faster pace of social change.

In fact, it comes to this: indirectly but nonetheless effectively for that, universities are forcing the pace of social change. While we in the universities feel a large responsibility to advance exact knowledge in all fields and to educate specialists, are we conscious of any comparably pressing obligation to study and to teach how society is to cope with accelerating social change, how technological developments, which threaten to get out of control, can help or hinder making this earth a garden for the human spirit, how individual character is to remain stable if everything else becomes fluid?

The present disaffection in a section of the student body can easily be exaggerated. It is marked enough, however, to show that something is seriously wrong. Is it not probable that, among other things, they are jarred by the pace of change and alarmed by the fluidity of any future they can see? They are suspicious of the business and political leaders who have negligently allowed technology to go on the loose, even if they have not indeed conspired to that end. So they want no part of the massive organizations, derisively called the establishment, that are omnipresent today. They suspect that the universities lack answers to the questions posed above, and in any large sense, they are right.

No one really knows how to control the social impact of the

massive organizations that use the new science and the new technology as the vehicle of their own advance. Universities can do something to explore the means and nourish the necessary spirit by giving much more attention to the study of man and society, aiming at a wider awareness of, and a deeper sensitivity to, civilized ends and purposes. If we are not providing this service for society, what case can we really make for freedom for the universities? If we do want to provide it at all adequately, we shall have to keep our priorities under review.

An argument for the need for balance between science and the social and humane studies is not a depreciation of the importance of science. The relentless probing of the mysteries of his world is a large part of the grandeur of man. Also, whether we talk of health, or relief from the drudgery of unending labour, or whatever, science has magnificent humane achievements to its credit. If not diverted by political upheaval, it will go on opening up new possibilities of a richer and nobler life. Acknowledging all this, it has to be remembered that all science can do is to create possibilities. The concern here is that a rate of scientific advance which outruns the capacity for social absorption of its discoveries will make its humane achievements irrelevant and frustrate the possibilities it opens up. If that happens, science too becomes irrelevant.

Science has no useful comment on the values by which men should live and relatively little to say on how they can or should organize themselves for the good life. It makes it possible for us to live more richly and humanely but does not tell us how to do it. In the international relations of this century, we have already had the object lesson. If we cannot learn how to live together on this globe, science will be turned to destructive horrors, and we shall all become playmates of the stars much sooner than we want to.

There are, therefore, pressing questions of priorities to consider. The universities must, and should, serve their society because they are a part of it and have everything at stake in its welfare and its sanity. That is why rapid social change without much sense of direction is so critical a matter. But service to society may be conceived in diverse ways. The public, governments, and even we ourselves sometimes, may conceive it too narrowly and look at the universities mainly as producers of knowledge, and of skilled manipulators of that knowledge, the market for which could be measured, the models prescribed, and production automated.

The broader conception pressed here is that the most essential service is to be moulders of men and women who get a vision of the good life and the good society from their universities. And if we are to talk in terms of production, a by-product of such service would be an enlarged constituency that understands clearly why universities need freedom in carrying on their work.

In conclusion, I would not want it thought that I overlook the occasion that brings us here today, the 125th anniversary of the commencement of teaching at Queen's University. Queen's has a proper pride in what it has done for more than a century in its devotion to teaching, often in strain and adversity but never lacking in spirit and resolution. I have not dwelt on the past because the future will not wait for us to do so. The biggest issues of the future affect all universities similarly, so the discussion has been general in its bearing and not particular. In particular, two things. First, an assertion: if Queen's University is to be true to its genius, it must go from strength to strength as a teaching institution. Second, an admission: in what I have been saying, I have not been free from the bias of long association with this University and the tradition of teaching, fearless inquiry, and loyal service to Canada which it has honoured for so long.

*Opening speech given as chairman of the Commit-
tee of Presidents of the Universities of Ontario in
Toronto, May 1968, to a meeting of the heads of
the various teaching departments of those universities. In 1966, the Spinks Commission on Graduate
Work in Ontario had recommended the establishment of a University of Ontario, on the model of
the University of California, as the only means of
achieving, among other things, the effective coordination of postgraduate work at the fifteen publicly
supported Ontario universities. The meeting was
called to launch a plan for coordinating postgraduate work voluntarily without the compulsion
that an overarching University of Ontario would
involve.*

Cooperation in Graduate Studies in Ontario Universities

On behalf of the Committee of Presidents, I welcome this distinguished company. I thank you for coming at the weekend, many of you from a long distance, to take part in this meeting. I justify asking you to come by saying that the business before us today is vitally important; indeed, I think it to be the most important business the universities of Ontario have yet attempted together.

We have known for some time that the days of *laissez-faire* in university education in Ontario are over. We have accepted this with good grace and have set about building a voluntary system of coordination in which we submit our graduate programmes to outside appraisal, share our library resources, and welcome visiting scholars from other universities within the system. We have adopted a common admission procedure and welcomed a uniform formula for operating grants. We are now cooperating in the search for a capital formula and are on the point of endorsing a systems approach to the sharing of computer facilities. In only one area—the coordination of

65

graduate studies—have we shrunk from grasping the nettle and weeding out any unnecessary and costly duplication, actual or potential, in graduate programmes. Today we have come here to grasp the nettle and clear the ground for a rational distribution of well-planned graduate programmes.

The urgent reasons for cooperation in the field of graduate studies are not far to seek. An obvious one is that, if the universities don't get together and do the job themselves, the government will step in and do it for them. The Minister of University Affairs alluded to this possibility in his Frank Gerstein lecture at York University in February 1966, when he said that "if the universities of Ontario failed to meet the responsibilities of the times, and if costly duplication of effort is evident, I cannot imagine that any society, especially one bearing large expense for higher education, will want to stand idly by. For there will be inevitably a demand—there have been indications of this in other jurisdictions—that governments move in and take over." I do not regard this statement as a threat to university autonomy. Rather, I take it as an expression of the inevitable consequence of our failure to order our affairs in a reasonable way. I do not say that we have yet failed. I do say we have not got as far forward as we should.

The financial constraints now facing the universities of Ontario push us strongly to cooperation in the expensive area of graduate studies. These constraints may not be unrelated to an impression in government circles that we have not done enough to put our houses in order. Anyway, there is growing evidence that the Government of Ontario, even with goodwill towards the universities and an announced intention to give the highest priority to education, is not going to find it politically feasible to give the universities all the money they consider necessary for their development as institutions which are to be at once first class, and equipped to do all that is attractive to them and worthwhile doing for its own sake. Some of us may think that the government is pursuing a short-sighted policy and is failing to realize that sums invested in the universities today will pay handsome dividends in accelerated economic growth in the future, that higher education is the best kind of investment open to us, and that the most important factor of production is brains. But the government has to face the electorate every four or five years and must in the nature of the democratic process, balance long-term benefits against immediate burdens. To be blunt about it, the universities, taken individually, will never have enough for all good purposes and so will be operating in conditions of scarcity. We must, therefore, accept the hard consequences of scarcity and learn how to make the maximum use of our scarce resources.

As I have just said, I do not think the universities of Ontario will have the means to continue developing as first-class institutions while at the same time pursuing a policy of self-sufficiency in which each counts on doing all that is attractive and well worth doing. So we face a choice. We can spread our scarce resources thinly in an effort at complete institutional independence of action while we sink down to second- or third-class status; or, on the other hand, we can aim at maintaining quality at the sacrifice of part of our self-sufficiency and some of our ambitions. Surely we must choose the latter course because no university worthy of the name would choose with its eyes open to be less than first class in what it offers. I do not think this latter alternative is as harsh as we fear. In Ontario, it is still open to each of us, in giving up some of our individual independence of action, to surrender it to the university system consisting of, and guided by, the universities themselves. It is greatly to the credit of the Government of Ontario that this is the course it would prefer us to take.

I wish I could say that the process of cooperation in the field of graduate studies will be a painless one, but I would be less than frank if I said it. All the universities will have to pass self-denying ordinances and curb their aspirations in some directions.

The older and more mature universities can take comfort that by and large cooperation will not require them to give up programmes of graduate studies already flourishing. Yet it will not do for them to say grimly, "Whatever we have, we hold." They will have to remember that cooperation and coordination cannot be wholly at the expense of the newer and smaller. To prevent that, the older and more mature will have to consider retraction in some fields of minimal commitment. If voluntary coordination is to work, there will have to be some sacrificing of interests and ambitions all around.

In the past, through lack of resources, Ontario universities perforce lagged in graduate studies, had to fill gaps in our needs for university teachers and research people by attracting both Canadians and immigrants who had got graduate degrees abroad. Over the past decade, the position has changed. Graduate programmes have been multiplied and extended in Ontario universities, and we are now well on the way to closing the gaps. Fortunately, as I said, there is little evidence that unnecessary duplication has yet reached alarming dimensions.

I hasten to say that short of concentrating all graduate study in one huge graduate school in the province, there is no escape from some duplication in many fields of study. Economics, history, chemistry, and physics are good illustrations. In the more esoteric fields, we probably ought to avoid all duplication. But what fields are esoteric in this degree will call for nice judgements. In between these two extremes, there will also be exquisite issues as to when duplication becomes wasteful because the decision will have to turn on guesses about future requirements as well as on present circumstances.

Our main task, however, will be not one of cutting back what already exists but of planning and coordinating future developments. Rapid as has been the growth of our graduate schools in recent years, most of their ordering and development is ahead of us. This year there are just under 9,000 full-time graduate students in the universities of Ontario. If the momentum we have now reached is continued, that number will more than double by 1975 and may triple by 1981.

Of course I do not know, nor do I think anyone else can carry conviction right now in saying, that we shall or shall not find such numbers of well-qualified persons seeking postgraduate education. It is perhaps also problematical whether we will have a need for such numbers of persons with postgraduate degrees. We do know we have been competing with one another pretty sharply in the last few years for the limited number of well-qualified Canadian graduate students, and have been taking significant numbers of non-Canadians to fill up available places. So the numbers of graduate students in 1975 and 1981 is somewhat speculative.

Planning and coordination will not come easily to us. It is commonplace that our domestic academic tradition has been highly individualistic. Both exhortation and example from highly respectable quarters have sold us on private enterprise. As Kenneth Hare said of universities in the first of his two Plaunt Lectures at Carleton University a year ago:

> I remember a picture, I think in the *New Yorker,* of the UN headquarters in New York with all the flags of the nations flying one way, except for one lonely flag pointing the other way. It was the flag of the Soviet Union,

68

but it might well have been that of Academe. We resist uniformity, change, external control, organization. We are not organization men, but cave-dwellers. And we are by nature competitive as societies, even tribal in characteristics. The mere thought that common action by our tribes in confederacy, like that of the Iroquois, might strengthen our hand, leaves us disdainful. Many of us will publicly deny this, but mentally admit it.*

I quoted earlier the Minister of University Affairs as telling us, in effect, that if the universities don't do the job the governments will do it for us. Now I should like to quote another passage from his Gerstein Lecture in 1966: "I am sure that to a very great extent the solution must lie in cooperation and coordination; in a willingness on the part of one university to share its facilities and, indeed, its staff, with students of another; in a willingness, as I have already noted, to share library facilities and materials; in a willingness, perhaps, to defer the entry into graduate work in given disciplines until such time as the overall demand would indicate that such expansion is required."

This then, is the task that confronts us. In taking it up, in graduate studies, Ontario will not be breaking entirely fresh ground. In 1962, eight universities in the Atlantic Provinces initiated the Atlantic Provinces Inter-University Committee on the Sciences with the object of concerting their efforts in the expensive scientific field. Some of the universities have decided to specialize in a B.Sc. or an honours B.Sc. programme, thinking that their educative efforts can best be focused within such a framework. Others wish to carry a limited programme at the master's level. Graduate work in the sciences, particularly at the doctoral and postdoctoral level, is concentrated on Dalhousie University in its Faculty of Graduate Studies and in engineering at the Nova Scotia Technical College.

In the United States the Committee on Institutional Cooperation, representing eleven Midwestern universities, was formed in 1958. The CIC operates a number of cooperative programmes: for example, a programme in biometeorology conducted on a resource-sharing basis. Under the current programme, students simply move from one campus to another taking courses or using laboratories and field facilities in which particular institutions have special strength. Another CIC initiative is a graduate-level programme of summer institutes in comparative literature designed to provide a strong

*Kenneth Hare, *On University Freedom in the Canadian Context* (Toronto: University of Toronto Press in association with Carleton University, 1968), p. 22.

pooling of resources and to open new research avenues for scholars in the field.

There are examples in the United States not only of cooperation among equals but also of smaller institutions which have established graduate programmes jointly with large universities nearby. Augustana College, Illinois, is offering a master's degree in earth science jointly with Iowa State University. Many colleges offer a three-year pre-engineering course in cooperation with a university graduate school. Princeton's special programme in Critical Language allows students from other colleges to transfer to its campus for a year. The University of Chicago offers a master's degree in one year through coordination of its programme with over twenty liberal arts colleges.

To the smaller universities in Ontario, which may be apprehensive that cooperation will tend to make them mere appendages of larger institutions, American experience shows that it is not always the big institution that possesses the distinctive programme or the prized facility. It is said that the finest telescope in the State of Missouri is located on the campus of Central Methodist College and its larger neighbours need not duplicate this expensive instrument.

So far, I have stressed the need for cooperation, expressed a preference for doing it voluntarily, and cited examples to show that it can be done. But I should be misleading if I gave the impression that there is nothing here but bitter pills to swallow. Cooperation and coordination have marked positive advantages. I have left them until now because I thought it better to offer a bracing chaser than to try to sugarcoat the pills themselves.

First, working together may enable us to do things that each of us working alone could not bring off. If one man has two left shoes and another man has two right shoes of the same size, design and colour as the first man's, each by himself will be a cripple; together, they can both run and not be wearied. To use an even more fitting example: if two neighbouring universities are both aspiring to graduate work in political science and in economics but neither has quite enough strength in either area to offer a programme at the graduate level, graduate work will have to be postponed at both places. But if they can work cooperatively, their strengths may complement each other. By pooling their resources, one may be able to offer a graduate programme in political science while the other undertakes graduate work in economics.

70

Here, then, are two programmes where none would otherwise have existed. Of course, this solution will not delight the two departments that are disappointed in their plans, even though these were essentially unrealizable. But they can take comfort from the fact that demand is growing and will continue to grow. Perhaps in the future there would be graduate programmes in both fields in both universities, unless, of course, all were swallowed up in the interval by behavioural psychology!

Cooperation may provide a small university with its only real chance of developing distinctive centres of excellence. Such an institution existing in the shadow of big neighbours may in circumstances of unrestricted competition find itself shut out of all the fields in which it might astutely equip itself to excel. The hard fact, of course, is that when new or developing fields are up for grabs, the older and larger universities can almost always take the risks of an initiative more quickly than can the newer and smaller. If, on the other hand, there is cooperation and big neighbours make some self-denying ordinances, as they must if voluntary coordination is to work, the smaller institution can hope to gain through some fresh thinking about new and exciting departures, and so be able to develop as *the* centre in particular fields in its region, if not in the whole province.

Interuniversity cooperation at the graduate level is necessary if we are to make optimum use of scarce resources. It has been shown to be feasible in other jurisdictions and we are encouraged to believe that it will be feasible in Ontario. Favourable developments, and continuing prospects of cooperation, in appraisals, the sharing of library research materials and computer facilities, and other cooperative ventures on which we are already embarked point that way.

Substantial progress along these lines at the graduate level will also, I think, be liberating for us all because our case for support in operating and capital grants will be so much the better. The vital concern of the whole community with continuing advance in higher education is understood in government circles and by many in the wider community. The advance will continue if we can give a good account of our stewardship.

So far I have been speaking as Chairman of the Committee of Presidents of the Ontario Universities, careful not to go beyond what my several colleagues would find themselves able to support. Seeing that I am almost at the end of my duties as Chairman, I should like now to speak only for myself, not worrying whether my colleagues will be with me or not.

There are fourteen universities in Ontario, all hopeful of staking out substantial ground for graduate studies. I do not think it is at all possible, in the near future, for the Province of Ontario to support fourteen flourishing graduate schools, with a substantial range of offerings at the Ph.D. level. Work at the M.A. or M.Sc. level, in many departments in all or most of these universities, may well be possible. I am speaking only about Ph.D. work, where the resources available will not make room for us all in any large way.

If we cannot divide up the field of graduate studies by agreement among ourselves, it is clear that the Government of Ontario will have to do it for us. It will not, of course, do it by specific allocation of the fields of graduate work among the several universities: the operating grants formula protects us from this horror. The effective way will be by pressure on the value of the basic unit in the formula. In our disappointment over the value of the basic unit for 1968/69, thus reducing the operating grants we had all hoped for, we have had the first instalment of this pressure. If misery loves company, then we should all be happy to know that we are all suffering because of *our* failure to divide up the field of graduate work among ourselves.

This division will be painful for us all, and there can be no escape from the pain. But we can choose what kind of pain we are to suffer. We can extend ourselves too ambitiously, and thus suffer from general anaemia. Alternatively, we can make some amputations at the extremities and/or go in for some mild feet-binding. I recognize that the pain may well be more severe for the newer and smaller universities. Several of the older are now well established and flourishing in a considerable range of graduate studies, and these should not be dismantled. Nevertheless, the still unsatisfied ambitions of these older institutions will have to be curbed, so there is pain for all, whether it affects three or four departments, or fifteen or sixteen departments.

Because the limiting of ambition is inescapable and affects us all, I have been trying to diagnose the distress and think of other ways of reducing the pain. If we could all accept the fact that undergraduate work of high quality is an honourable estate, cultivation of which gives us dignity and an opportunity to stretch ourselves and test our powers, we would find the inevitable restraints much easier to take. Undergraduate teaching is an honourable estate. I spent most of my life at it and never felt underprivileged or reduced to second-rate citizenship. Most of my contemporaries had the same preoccupations and did not find themselves frustrated or demeaned. Why can't we accept this now?

The answer comes quickly in a chorus: we cannot get or keep good staff unless we give them the assurance of sharing in graduate work and significant research. All university teachers, actual or potential, we are told, think it a shabby existence if they are not deep in graduate work and research. It is important to ask why.

I grant at once that to be a good teacher one must be alive in his subject: he must be studying and exploring beyond and around the subjects he teaches, but I am not sure he needs to be attended by a cloud of graduate students to do this. I grant also that the situation has changed because a substantial number of outside granting bodies, catering mainly to the natural and applied sciences, will now stake university teachers to explore the frontiers of knowledge, but will not offer them support merely to make them better teachers. In these sciences, no doubt, there is a more intimate connection between graduate work and research and high quality teaching than in other fields of instruction. But even here the closeness of the connection is often exaggerated by the zealous promoters of graduate work and research.

However, there is much more to the mania about graduate work that is attributable to the universities themselves and not to the ambitions of members of university staffs or to the policy of outside agencies. We have allowed, indeed encouraged and even driven, members of staff to believe that recognition, advancement, salary increases, and promotions depend on involvement with graduate students and associated research, and the publication of papers on abstruse subjects. I believe we are all guilty of this, although I have fought against it in the best way I know. I have said repeatedly to my teaching colleagues at Queen's University that I would not give any preference in promotion and salary increases to active researchers and supervisors of graduate students as against the good teacher of undergraduate students who lacked both graduate students and research papers. The almost invariable retort to this determination was that I could not succeed because heads of departments and deans of faculties would defeat me and even if this policy should have some success at Queen's University, other universities would not follow it. The blunter members of staff would tell me that it was imperative for them to maintain mobility, not because they wanted to leave Queen's University as soon as they could get decent offers, but because they were convinced that offers from other institutions improved immensely their chances for promotion and gratifying salary increases at home.

There is too much truth in what I was told for us to be able to ignore it. While we cannot ignore it, I think we could cope with it cooperatively by agreeing among ourselves that we would take great pains to see that the encouragements offered to good undergraduate teachers were at least as good as those given to members of staff who were heavily committed to graduate students and research. Indeed, I believe that if we could agree on such a policy and stick to it, we would find many staff members shouting with relief. Many of them would welcome freedom from the bore of helping second- and third-rate graduate students over the hurdles, and of supervising their dreary theses. Many would welcome freedom to improve their own education in breadth instead of grubbing away underground in depth research. Much of the mystique that surrounds graduate work would disappear.

What grounds have I for believing this? Admittedly, the belief is partly based on a hunch that educated men and women don't really want to be as narrowly specialized for so much of their time as now happens in this dispensation. But my view rests partly on inferences that I think cogent. I have seen something of the array of research projects coming before granting bodies, especially in the humanities and social sciences. Proud researchers send me copies of their work. I skim these and others that appear in learned journals, and again and again I ask myself: why did he choose this subject? There have seemed to me to be three main possibilities. First, his supervisor in graduate school dug him down into this deep hole: he doesn't know how to get out, so he runs lateral horizontal shafts off the main shaft without ever getting up for air or sunshine. Second, he is in a state of frantic desperation to find *some* topic for research so that he can get out a paper to impress the head of his department and others, because he thinks that this is the only way to impress the powerful. The third possibility is the most alarming: his appointment to a teaching position in a university was a disastrous mistake. He is so dull and unimaginative, so little sensitive to the grandeur and misery of the human enterprise and to the larger mysteries of the world we live in, that he could not possibly interest intelligent students.

It is here that I get clues to the rising disaffection and incipient rebellion of intelligent undergraduates. Too often they are being short-changed because their teachers, preoccupied with graduate studies and narrow, specialized research, have disabled themselves for effective undergraduate teaching.

So, I should like to urge that, when the heads of departments of the several universities gather this afternoon, and again later in successive meetings, they do not focus solely on the narrow issue of rationalization of the distribution of graduate teaching and research. There is grave danger that such focusing will be sterile. Each department head has to remember his duty to protect departmental interests and ambitions and the talk may quickly be reduced to haggling. He has to reckon with reproaches from his dean and his president, to whose ambitions Machiavelli's dictum is relevant: "Mankind never knows when to limit its hopes." I trust that department heads will move at least part of the time on a plane of common interests where there is room for us all in the development of excellence and the realization of worthy ambitions, the plane of undergraduate teaching.

It would be liberating for us all if we could agree on reassurances about promotions and salary increases for those who would be content, or even eager, to be good undergraduate teachers, bringing breadth as well as depth to their teaching. On the whole we would have happier colleagues, fewer disgruntled students, and a better posture for our common case to the Government of Ontario for operating grants.

I don't think I underestimate the difficulties. I could talk about them at great length; for example, we would have to change both the attitudes and the regulations of outside granting bodies. We would have to think seriously about modifying the kind of advanced study suitable for persons who want appointments to university teaching staffs. These difficulties look formidable largely because we have not given thought and ingenuity to how to meet them. We have now reached the point where we can no longer indulge slack-mindedness on these matters. I think we can get further on the lines I am suggesting than by limiting ourselves to any narrower focus. If we really believe in the ancient and honourable role of universities in cultivating the minds of the young, why should we lock ourselves in impoverished struggle about strips of narrow ground in graduate studies when broad acres are open to us all in undergraduate teaching?

Convocation address at St. Francis Xavier University, May 1968. Financial dependence of the universities on governments was deepening year by year. There was evidence that the public was becoming restive about skyrocketing university expenditures and about hostile intransigence of groups of students at many universities. The question as to how universities were to maintain their essential autonomy in the face of such needs and pressures seemed to be growing critical.*

Universities, Government, and the Public

To talk about the relations of universities and governments is to take up a very delicate matter. Government is a collective organization for carrying out indispensable functions. One of its main jobs is to maintain order, and for that purpose it holds a monopoly of coercive power, to be applied crudely under the law if need be. It exists also to mediate and settle disputes between different sections of the community, to see that inevitable social change is an orderly process. Democratic governments achieve this essentially by compromise, which is almost always a second or third best, accepted for the sake of peace and well worth the price. Government also exists to provide a wide range of services desired by various sections of its citizens. Who gets these services and how much of them is also settled not on the basis of a perfect solution but a tolerable compromise. It is, so someone has said, a substitute for civil war, and I would say a very civilized substitute indeed. But the only activity carried on within it that approaches the perfection of the ideal is statesmanship, and sometimes it falls short on that too.

Universities, on the other hand, do not hold the bludgeon of power. Nor are they driven to compromise or capitulation for the sake of

*Published in *Queen's Quarterly*, LXXV, No. 3 (Autumn 1968).

peace, at least not until the last two or three years. They provide services directly to some sections of the people, and indirectly to all, but their highest service is to reason and truth on which no compromise is possible. In contrast to governments, it is not their service to seek and embrace the tolerable mean between the high-minded and the low-minded, but rather, within their proper sphere, to aim at the ideal and approach the perfect—however short of the target they may fall in practice. In somewhat haughty fashion sometimes perhaps, they build ivory towers and dreaming spires so as to stand above the trafficking of the forum and the market place.

In recent years, for reasons that need no telling here, universities have become deeply dependent on governments. Governments and society have become just as deeply dependent on universities. In substance, both are in partnership, and what ill-assorted partners they are! The partnership is an uneasy one, and must, in the nature of things, continue as such. (That is why talk about their relations is a very delicate matter.) Universities worry because their powerful partner can wreck them, one or all. Governments think the partnership very unequal: universities have all the freedom and government is responsible for all the debts. Yet they are not wholly alien and out of sympathy. Some university staff members seem to me to be natural-born politicians who have missed their calling. I have sometimes glimpsed ministers and civil servants thinking appreciatively and wistfully of the ivory tower.

To come back to the university, it has meaning only as it supports and nourishes the life of the mind. Mind can thrive and renew itself only if it is free to range, to inquire without hindrance, and to report what it finds. The only minds we know, of course, are individual minds, and they can be free outside universities as well as inside, but on one condition, that there are social supports and buttresses for that freedom. (Here, I think, I state one particular of a universal truth: the fate of all enterprise of individual persons of whatever kind is bound up in the collectivities of which they are a part. They cannot find the energy or the tools to cut sharply across the grain of their society for very long.)

So, if the university has any meaning, any distinctive and vital significance, it is as a buttress to freedom of the mind, "to follow knowledge like a sinking star, beyond the utmost bound of human thought." The university is a collectivity. We do not need to be told that *universitas*, in the Middle Ages, was first a generic name for an association, a corporation which sought to guarantee rights and privileges for its members against feudal lords, and even from strenuous clerics, the burly rogues of the time, arbitrary and powerful men who kept Europe tottering on the edge of anarchy. The university of masters and scholars, when it came, wanted to guarantee continuity of inquiring, teaching, and learning, and also to provide a defence against the outer world for men engaged in learning.

This is the rock from which we are hewn, however neglectful or unheeding of this original mission universities have been, or are today. They, more than any other organization, have kept the traditions alive, and they are the best prospects for buttressing the free life of the mind. Of course, they may fail.

Indeed, they will fail if we decide that security for the free-ranging mind can safely be left to the universities without further thought or worry. Of this we do need reminding. There will be no autonomy or independence for the university unless the larger collectivities grasp its value and support its central purpose. To put it simply, Canadian universities cannot and will not retain their autonomy for their essential purposes unless Canadian society sees that autonomy as vital for the welfare of our country and is fully apprised of what is needed to secure it. More concretely, the universities of Nova Scotia or Ontario or elsewhere in Canada will not hold their freedom unless large sections of public opinion in the provinces are alert and vigilant for their protection.

The only security the universities have is in public opinion, and we should be doing much more than we are to win and hold its allegiance. We need to build support patiently on a wide front by showing that the interests of the universities and the community run side by side. It is not necessary, I am sure, to enforce the point, or to stress the effort required, in this university which knows from its own experience and accomplishments that vital movements have to be organized upwards and cannot be called into life and vigour by pious talk at the top.

Generally speaking, we are reluctant to learn this lesson. We have seen in the last decade, in greater or lesser degree in all provinces, how the universities can be liberated by large financial support from governments, and we are anxious to believe that liberation in still larger measure will come from that source. Of course, we are not unaware of the dangers of large dependence on governments. To escape these dangers, we have counted largely on mechanics of organization, bemused by the example of the University Grants Commission in Britain, and by refinements of that example in the way of formulas for determining levels and distribution of government grants. The British University Grants Commission has been our model and, in our minds, an adequate mainstay. Watching it for a long time, we concluded that an independent commission standing as a buffer between governments and universities would secure the support and ward off the dangers.

It was a civilized means and an effective instrument as long as university grants took a relatively small part of government budgets and were not seen to threaten other powerful bodies and blocs of opinion that have a stake in wide access to the public purse. But that day has vanished as new universities are established, as higher education perforce becomes more complex and more expensive, and costs rise in what seems astronomical fashion. It is clearly gone when public concern over university costs leads the Public Accounts Committee in Britain to insist on the auditing of university accounts, a pointless exercise unless that body is preparing to say that too much is spent on this or that. Perhaps, for all I know, too much is spent on this or that, but the Public Accounts Committee is not qualified to say what is too much on this or on that.

An agreed formula for determining the level of operating grants in a university system and then distributing them to the several universities is a mechanism for avoiding the dangers of line-by-line budgeting or auditing. But everything still depends on the value put on the basic unit in the formula. It would be naive to expect any government, dependent on public opinion, to give any independent agency like a grants commission power to fix that value at a level that compelled it either to alienate the taxpayer by its general level of taxation or severely to disappoint influential interests with heavier voting power than universities can command and with other ideas about how public money should be spent.

It is clear enough in the last few months that we are approaching this crunch in more provinces than one. And there is no point in railing at governments for being sensitive to these pressures, beyond arguing that public opinion is being misread, that ripples of irritation are being mistaken for groundswells of deep protest. The logic of our democratic system requires governments to attend to public opinion and none of us really wants it otherwise. We had better recognize too that our governments are responding to demands for social justice, to be served, one hopes, by redistribution of income through the treasury. We should also appreciate the heavy risk that large bodies of opinion will put social justice (in the health and welfare fields, to take only two examples) ahead of mounting support to universities, and perhaps even of university autonomy.

If we are questioned about the justice of providing an expensive education at substantially less than cost to a preferred group of the young so that they can enjoy high social status and income for the rest of their lives, have we ready and convincing answers? And even if we have good answers and explanations, will they carry conviction in the face of a highly vocal (although, as I believe, numerically very small) group of students who think that the universities are still doing less than enough for them?

Let me take pains here not to be misunderstood. First, I do not believe that the question posed above puts exclusive and inescapable alternatives. Of course, there are people with a passion for justice who will place its claims above individual freedom, including freedom of the mind, and above a liberating autonomy for universities. But I believe that if we order our general public affairs with enough intelligence and ingenuity we can have a fair measure of both. Second, I believe that a society that puts an exquisite social justice above the claims of the free-ranging mind, its nurture and education, will end by losing both. This, I believe, is especially true for the urban industrialized society that is coming to dominate our social landscape. If we are to keep its complexities from bringing us to paralysis, we must have great resources of highly educated intelligence as well as good will and passion for justice. We must have these resources not only to manage the productive apparatus of our society efficiently but, even more, to keep its rigidities, regional disparities, and imbalances under constant review. We must be continually watchful of the propensity of our burgeoning technology to get out of hand and to debauch or destroy essential human values. We desperately need social critics who are not only repelled by the impersonality of our massive productive apparatus and its materialism, but who also understand how it ticks and how to defend the human spirit against its assaults.

Rightly understood then, the free university protecting the free minds within it is not in competition with the claims of justice, but an indispensable ally in the refining of justice in a complex society. The *status quo* must be kept under constant review. That can only be done effectively by educated intelligence imbued with the tradition of Western humanism. If universities do not prepare such minds, no other organization will.

No one should underestimate the difficulty of getting widespread public acceptance of this as the most essential function of the universities. Everyone can understand readily enough the argument that heavy support for universities is needed to prepare scientists, doctors, technicians, managers and the like, to run the economy, to raise productivity, improve health and provide more leisure. Universities are doing this, and will continue to do it, and I do not quarrel with that at all. But perhaps we have oversold this particular role to the public and to the government, leading them to think of the university as a utility, a factory for machining tools for the productive system.

Actually, a lot of this professional-technical education has little necessary relation to the releasing of minds to range with utter freedom. Much of it has been done about as well in the Soviet Union where autonomy of universities is not thought indispensable. If governments come to believe that the servicing of the society with useful components for the productive machine is the universities' main job, then they cannot be expected to pay too much attention when we scream, "Hands off!" We will have oversold this particular argument.

For holding the allegiance of one particular section of the university constituency of great importance we have indeed oversold it. The universities draw large numbers of questing idealistic students. Some of them—I do not know how many, but clearly there are more of them year by year—have decided that the universities are the handmaidens of the establishment, the business and corporate élite, not only serving the *status quo* but using the educative process and university resources to clamp its grasp more tightly on us. Some of these young people are intoxicated, some of them deeply shaken, by the discovery that man and the world are mysteries. They want all the adventures of the mind in probing the mystery—and of the tongue in talking about it—and they find their university too much preoccupied with the mundane and the immediate. They are potential allies for defending the citadel. In most universities, we are not responding enough to their freshness and eagerness, so numbers of them become disaffected rebels, talking seriously about setting up anti-universities and anti-curricula. Disaffected because frustrated, they become unreasonable, indulge in sit-ins, break-ins, indecencies, practise violence in the name of pacifism, and so on.

Nothing could be better calculated to disenchant the public with the universities. Why should vast sums be poured into institutions that cannot maintain internal order? What credence do you give organizations that talk about the free play of the mind and then are dishonoured by a free display of the fists? What do you make of bodies that talk about submitting everything to reason and are seen to be submitting to threats and riots?

The problem of the university today is not only to ensure that reason prevails in its affairs, but also that reason is seen to prevail. This means meeting the demand for participation in the reasoning process by all members of the collectivity including the students. It does not mean yielding to so-called student power. It does mean enlisting the creative, energetic idealism of students as persons interested in the future of their university and not just in consuming what the university has to offer at the moment. The recognition of legitimate student aspirations for this larger role in university affairs is often troubling to graduates of earlier days and is often misinterpreted as "softness" in the face of power-play tactics. The university must be firm in resisting the latter. But it must show its sympathy for this larger role before strong-arm tactics get the support of more than the small minority of students who care only for the power game and have no real interest in the university. Making the public understand what sometimes looks to an outsider like a wavering, ambivalent stand on student participation is only one facet of the problem of explaining ourselves to the public, but it illustrates well the kind of problem involved.

There are many other facets I shall not touch here. All I could say would reinforce the argument that to keep the wider public in sympathy with the universities and keenly aware of how fully the long-term interests of society and the universities run side by side will require the support of all the friends the universities have. Their chief friends and best interpreters are their graduates. Fom those to whom much has been given much is to be expected.

Convocation address at McGill University in October 1968, just after Dr. Corry's retirement from the principalship of Queen's University. During the 1967–1968 sessions of the Canadian universities, the demands of the activist students had continued to mount. The insistent claims were for large student representation on boards of governors, senates, and various academic committees, a weighty share in setting programmes of studies, and freedom to decide what specific courses they should take and how these should be taught.

Anxious Concern, Vague Unease

The raw facts that have just been given about me are accurate enough. I have had nearly fifty years of unbroken association with universities as a student and teacher, and in other more questionable roles. Now, having sloughed off responsibility, having outlived duty except for such fragments as still attach to a visiting professor, I should not be inhibited in saying what I think. But I do find myself under a new restraint. Those who have neither responsibility nor duty in the premises should not give much unsolicited counsel or gratuitous advice. So, as I refer to some of the changes I have seen and to their likely consequences, I shall try not to be dogmatic about how to deal with these consequences. As you know, this will not be easy for one accustomed to the oracular manner of a university principal.

For most of my time, the universities were cloistered institutions. They went their own way with little public interest or attention. They were left alone to struggle along in poverty. As in social life generally, poverty provided its own internal discipline. There was very little open disaffection inside and almost no interference from the outside. There was no significant challenge to the authority of their constituted officers or governing bodies. There were, of course, occasional exceptions at particular times and in particular institutions, but not often and not many.

Recently there has been a sudden and long overdue recognition of the importance of the universities and a correspondingly rapid improvement in their public support. They have enjoyed, if that is the right word, an enormous rise in prestige. Even if they are not all things to all men they are being treated as if they were. The slightest flutter inside one of them is front-page news.

But, of course, this has its consequences. The internal discipline enforced by poverty has greatly weakened. Factions of both staff and students challenge constituted authority. This should not be surprising. Revolutions are not made by the oppressed and disinherited. Generally speaking, they are made by the rising classes, dissatisfied with their rate of rise. And both university staff and students are rising classes. It doesn't take a long memory to realize that.

Also, in this same period, the universities have become much larger and more complex, with growing problems of internal communication and adjustment. Inevitably, their internal politics become much more intense, and potentially explosive. Even if universities were not sedately conservative by nature, the insistent pressures of their remarkable expansion in the last decade would have taxed severely their capacity to adjust themselves fast enough to rapid change.

These are good enough explanations of the turmoil universities are in, but they don't wash us clean in the eyes of the public. Here is an irony I had not expected to see. Just as the public importance of universities is handsomely recognized and the scale of public support given them frees them from the limitations imposed by poverty in the past, their ability to govern themselves in good order comes in question. Neither governments nor the taxpayers to whom they must answer think well of heavy commitments for vital public purposes to organizations that, on the surface at any rate, appear to be internally unstable.

Even without the added provocation of internal instability, the temptation for governments to intervene will be strong. Encouraging precedents for such action are ready to hand. Higher education is now an industry affected by a public interest. All such industries sooner or later have come under governmental regulation. It will be disastrous indeed if constituted authority in the university, under challenge from within, is also overridden from without.

86

In most Canadian universities substantial adjustments to meet changed conditions are under way. In particular, a moderate re-constitution of constituted authority is nearly everywhere well advanced. What is imperatively needed now is firmness of authority and loyalty to it, a trial of the revised arrangements in good faith and observance of due process in pressing for further change. Failing that, there is heavy risk of government intervention which will undermine the essential freedom of the universities and advantage no one, unless it be a few extremist students who really want to destroy the universities.

The most important decisions to be taken in a university are what shall be taught in it. Traditionally, each university, within its resources, decided what fields of knowledge it would offer instruction in and how particular fields would be segmented for the purpose. In genuinely free universities, once these choices had been made, the individual instructor decided what the content of his courses would be and how they would be taught. This was the essence of the freedom of the teacher: no one worth his salt would stay indefinitely in a place that prescribed what and how he should teach in the courses allotted to him.

Consumers' choice then was limited to choosing the university and the faculty or school in which the student wanted to be instructed. Knowledge was thought to confer authority over what to teach and how. Today this dimension of authority is also being challenged in greater or less degree. A minority of students wants a large voice in what they shall be taught and how. What change in circumstances brings this demand to the fore? Under what provocation do students come to make a claim of this kind?

Again I invoke the memory of the ancients forty years ago. Decisions on what to teach were much simpler then because not nearly so many choices were open. In many subjects—not all, but many— our knowledge was limited. There was a core, or what was believed to be a core, of knowledge. If you moved far afield from that, you were outtalking your information. In the subjects I began to teach then, there were one or two text books giving general surveys, and relatively little periodical literature. There were, of course, other books that had a relation to the subject taught. But that relation was not obvious, its relevance had to be established by the lecture. In that day, duplicate copies of these books and materials were luxuries not often found; the lavish duplicating services of today did not exist.

For these reasons, the formal lecture, competently handled, had a central place. It was the only way, in many subjects, to blend the ingredients in the dish of knowledge, to give them spice and flavour, to make the dish palatable, or even in some cases, digestible. In the hands of the masters, it was a highly artistic performance.

Much has changed in the interval. There has been a continuing and accelerating proliferation of knowledge. Endless books and a vast periodical literature expound that knowledge at length. Many specialized fields of knowledge have been developed, branching off into subspecialties, each of which can be made a separate subject of study. The student with some curiosity quickly learns what a range of possibilities there are. When the teacher in the formal lecture determines what the fare is to be, the student knows there is much more that could be taken up, much of which, he thinks, would have more interest and relevance to him. Accordingly, increasing numbers of students, when presented with the *table d'hote* menu, want to choose *à la carte*.

When faced with such demands, the teacher is under some embarrassment. He knows there is other matter he could expound as part of the course. It is harder than it used to be for him to say that his responsibility is to the central core, the illuminating principles, the coherent logic that relates the content of his course to other branches of knowledge.

Students can say that these principles and that logic are expounded in a large literature, and that they can read and summarize as well as he can. Worse still, many subjects of instruction now are out on the periphery at the growing points of knowledge and take the core for granted. Somebody else has the responsibility for expounding on the core.

So, the embarrassment of riches does make it more difficult to be convincing on what to teach; hence the need to respond to student interest in curriculum and course content by consultation and explanation. If the teacher cannot reach students where they now are, he has no hope at all of bringing them where he now is. No doubt a good many adjustments on the formal side of instruction will show themselves desirable through consultation. But any large recognition of consumers' choice has forbidding difficulties. Of course, the consumers would choose variously and, lacking the discipline of a price system, the result would be paralyzing confusion.

It would not only be confusion, it would be betrayal of the essential role of the universities, which is to transmit a heritage of knowledge and a discipline of learning. The things of the mind are subtle and fragile, easily slid over, fragmented and lost. Occasional geniuses conquer a subject quickly and find its relatedness to other knowledge easily, but for nearly all of us the road to learning has been hard to find and follow through many patches of rough terrain, and our passage marked by sweat and tears, self-doubt and even despair. We need the firm assurance of a continuing institution that the way to the coveted vistas on the heights does indeed lead through this hard country. No one needs this assurance more than a generation whose experience, for the most part, suggests that the good things of life come easily.

Any widespread recognition of consumers' choice in formal instruction threatens the honourable status of the teacher and undermines his authority in the classroom. He would cease to be the chef to whose knowledge, skill, and artistry we commit ourselves and become instead the waiter who takes the orders and carries in the dishes. Hack-writers, who write to order, are almost always dreary. Hack-professors would be still worse.

Even if it is said, as it will no doubt be said, that much of our teaching lacks artistry and imagination, that there are not enough genuine chefs and too many hash-slingers, that is not a ground for concessions that will debase teaching, and give, by contrast, still more glitter to research, supervision of graduate students, and consulting work. The chief way to maintain the authority of the teacher in the classroom is by indirection, by exalting the status of the teacher as teacher, by proving that we believe the most honourable career in a society is the teaching of the young. And, if we cannot halt just now the general obsession about power, then let us celebrate what Justice Holmes called "the subtle and postponed power" that comes only to the thinker and the teacher, the assurance that even after he himself has passed from the scene, men and women will still be moving to the measure of his thought and teaching.

How good it would be to stop here on this high note with this counsel of perfection! However, it is empty talk that does not concern itself with ways and means. More must be said. However, I cannot say more in general without making some distinctions and sharpening the focus.

The present-day university is a house of many mansions. There is teaching, graduate and undergraduate; there is research which, if not taken obsessively, enlivens teaching. Then there are the various fields of teaching and research: the sciences, pure and applied, the professional schools, the humanities and social sciences. In each of those fields, there are, in varying proportion, two principal kinds of students and two principal kinds of teachers, one lot whose interest and decisive bent is for study in depth while the other is drawn to study in breadth, the microscopic and the macroscopic, those who are fascinated by the trees and those who want to scan the forest.

This division of bent and interest is not a clear-cut one, but it will stand in general. There are, of course, the Einsteins, the Toynbees, and the de Chardins, pearls without price, and also lesser fry who try. They are still exceptions to the two broad categories. The division is not determined by level of intelligence, as protagonists on both sides say reproachfully. I put it down mainly to the elusive thing we call temperament, and I make no sweeping judgement. It takes all kinds of people to make a world, and nearly all kinds to make a university, as we conceive it.

In the last three centuries, we have had enormous success in penetrating the secrets of nature with the microscope, taking it as the symbol for probing in depth. That success is at the root of nearly everything that has transformed the world our great-grandfathers knew. Bemused by that success, universities in the last fifty years shifted their perspectives and altered their priorities, giving first place to studies in depth.

The success and the prestige of the natural and applied sciences gained by probing in depth, have affected the humanities and social sciences in a marked way. They hope for similar results and recognition through being scientific and microscopic. All teaching in all subjects has gained in depth by these methods, usually at the expense of breadth. Nearly all graduate work is dominated by the urge to probe deeper and deeper. The Ph.D. mill is more congenial to those whose bent is for depth. A high proportion of those who go through it come out with the indelible stamp of the specialist. It is from the product of this mill that nearly all university teachers are now being selected. I need not say how much the younger staff have been encouraged by the universities to keep up their specialties and go on probing in depth. In perspective and priorities, the universities have been committing themselves heavily to highly specialized education.

If we are thinking only about the advancement of knowledge, the advantages of this bias are not open to dispute, at least in the short run. If we are thinking about the best service to the teaching func-

90

tion of the universities, there are several questions to be raised. Here I touch only one of these questions. The bias I have been speaking of runs strong and has powerful momentum, but it runs counter to another trend, I would say a marked trend, in the interest of students away from the particular and microscopic, away from the materialist and scientific towards the general and the philosophical. Whether this trend of student interest will persist and strengthen cannot be predicted with certainty. I take it seriously because I believe it will.

At present, at any rate, growing numbers of students are looking critically at the world we have created with the aid of science and technology. It is a complex interdependent world whose massive apparatus sometimes seems to be getting beyond human control, and they don't like it. They overlook, of course, one of its important by-products, the high standard of living and relative affluence which they take for granted. Leave that aside; they dismiss it as irrelevant. They find the incessant social change associated with our world dehumanizing. It tears people from their roots, breaks down the sense of community, leads to loneliness and anonymity. They despair of a humane way of life in the mass society. They believe rightly that ceaseless preoccupation with science and technology will aggravate the malaise.

The mounting distress of the great cities everywhere shows that this anxiety is not fanciful. It is shared by more than students: indeed it is shared by all those who know what is going on and have any imagination. There is a large pessimism in the air about the future, a sense that something has gone wrong with our values, our notion of the meaning and purpose of life, that our mechanisms for social adjustment do not enable us to control our destiny any more. We have begun to ask why.

The group of students referred to a few minutes ago are asking why very insistently. That is to say, the interest moves from the scientific to the human, from the infinitely small to the large, to the philosophical, from depth to breadth. It is surely ominous that, on the outer fringes, there is much talk about a new religion, or giving a new face to old religions, because that is what happens in societies that despair of a good life in the here and now. It seems preposterous that, given all our command over the means of life, we should get ourselves into this fix. But there it is. We do not know how widespread the anxious concern, the vague unease, really is. There is little evidence that it has cut deeply with students in the sciences, natural or applied. The professional schools seem relatively unaffected. The stir is mostly in the humanities and social sciences, which no doubt are now recruiting the students most vulnerable to this kind of concern. My intimate knowledge is confined to the humanities and social sciences, so perhaps my comments are drawn from an unrepresentative sample. However, this group of disciplines is the one where the authority of the teacher in the classroom is likely to get the most serious challenge, and what I say now is restricted to them and to undergraduate instruction.

Student revolt, student unease—and the unease is much more widespread than the open revolt—the concern with curriculum and course content in the humanities and social sciences, have come mainly because the dominating interest of staff and university has been going one way while the most vocal, and much of the most lively, student concern is going another way. To the extent that this is so, the authority of the teacher in the classroom will remain under question. For his only authority is a moral authority, valid because it is generally accepted.

Here again I must particularize. Presumably, there is no problem of acceptance in the highly specialized courses and seminars open only to students who have made their commitment to the specialty, made their choice for probing in depth. Nor is it proper or necessary that all courses open to the generality of students should be turned into bull sessions that confront the universe head-on. Bull sessions are wonderful, but they are, by nature, informal and cannot be systematic. There will still be many students who want educated skills, covet precise mastery in particulars. What is needed, I believe, in most of our universities is a fuller response to the rapidly growing student interest in studies in breadth. In the face of the proliferation of specialties, there should be stronger affirming and delivering on the obligation to offer a general liberal education, taking very special care to bring knowledge, insight, and analysis to bear systematically on the nature and destiny of man and his perplexities in the second half of the twentieth century.

Admittedly, a university cannot claim to be honouring another of its obligations, to offer a searching view of knowledge, unless many of its teachers are charged with elucidating specialties in depth. But we need desperately that more teachers of specialties should take greater pains to show the relation and the significance of their specialty to the anxieties that affect contemporary life. If teachers cannot reach down to where the student now is and make contact

92

with what he knows and what he imagines and fears, his respect cannot be gained by talking over his head about complex detail. Conversely, there will be respect for mastery in a specialty that turns revealing beams of light on the general human situation. There is no better way, perhaps no other way, of exposing the delusion that those who don't know what there is to be learned should be determining what shall be taught.

Restoring general liberal education to primacy, or let us say parity, will not be easy because it means considerable reshuffling of priorities in the use of resources and in the preoccupations of many members of staff, more premiums for inspired teaching of undergraduates, and perhaps fewer for research, publication, and guidance of graduate students. There is also an issue of good faith for universities, they having encouraged members of staff to prepare for one kind of duty then ask them to take up a substantially different kind of duty. More than that, it is likely that many persons who have had the Ph.D. drill are temperamentally unsuited for teaching with the kind of emphasis I have been talking about. I took careful note of this difficulty earlier. One will not get skill and enthusiasm in teaching that has to cut across the grain of bent and temperament. So, it will not be easy.

Indeed, if I am anywhere near right in diagnosis, it will be necessary to reconsider with great care the kind of postgraduate education offered to persons wanting to prepare themselves for teaching posts in the humanities and social sciences. In their preparation, shouldn't there be still more firming up and enlarging of their grasp of existing knowledge, more pondering of the dilemmas of the human situation, and less emphasis on original research that too often has no relevance to anything likely to happen to us "on this bank and shoal of time"? If, as I suspect, this is what is needed, it will take time. But universities dare not shrink from what is necessary to meet their obligation to general liberal education on the grounds that it is painful and takes too much time. For no one else will give that education, so badly needed in our day.

Convocation address at the University of Windsor in October 1968. The remarks were provoked by widespread assertions, paraded as self-evident, that one cannot be a good teacher unless one is deep in original research.

Crisis in Teaching

In the last ten years, the universities of Canada have been marking their progress by crises or, more correctly perhaps, by accumulating crises. First, there was the crisis of numbers, then the crisis of finance, now the crisis of student disaffection. I am tempted now to announce the crisis of teaching. Maybe crisis is too strong a word, overstates the trouble. However, universities are involved in so many crises that it is hard to get them to attend to anything that isn't a crisis. First things must come first, they say. So I say loudly, "Crisis."

To me, there is not much overstatement in saying "crisis," because I believe that more students are uneasy and dissatisfied about the state of undergraduate teaching, particularly in the humanities and social sciences, than over any other single matter. I realize fully, of course, that many dissatisfied students use teaching as a whipping boy, venting on it what would be seen, if analyzed, to be dissatisfaction with themselves, chagrin at finding there is no royal road to learning, discomfort at being round pegs in square holes, and so on.

But that is not the whole thing by any means. A critic of teaching performance in Britain put the revealing question the other day.

When university staff members say resolutely, "Now I must get back to my own work," how many of them mean the teaching or preparation for the teaching of undergraduate courses, and how often do they mean it? The answer to this question in Canada is, "Not many, and not nearly often enough," I am sure. Education in universities—and that means teaching—is tending to become the servant of scholarship and research instead of being at least its equal. This is what makes the crisis.

I do not put heavy blame in all this on members of university staffs. "My own work," as the phrase goes, is nearly always creditable, honourable, and important: original research, publication, supervision of graduate students, and so on. All that is at stake is priorities, or more accurately, whether enough staff members give enough of their best and freshest attention to undergraduate teaching. Given the variety of time-consuming chores that have had to be passed over to members of staff by their universities, it is hard to keep duties in balance. Indeed, in the emerging pattern of priorities, the universities themselves have a large responsibility. In their general policy and allocation of resources, nearly all of them have been moving—some faster, some slower—towards putting the advancement of knowledge ahead of undergraduate teaching. These shifts have not always been made deliberately. Generally they have been made piecemeal in response to heavy pressures very hard to resist in these last days. Such blame as there is must be distributed. In a time of very severe staff shortages, prospective staff members are in a seller's market. They are in a position to enforce their own strong preferences. And many of them have such preferences, fastened on them by the graduate schools from which they come, preferences that do not rank undergraduate teaching highly.

Regardless of who is to blame and how much, I believe this emerging priority is wrong, that the first duty of the universities is to give high-quality general undergraduate education. If our complex society is to meet its problems and retain its sanity, we need to leaven the public with large numbers of persons of good general education, with critical minds, deeply aware of the distresses that come when we do not know what to do with our leisure and relative affluence, sensitive to the puzzles of reconciling order and individual dignity in a mass society, alert to the rich promise as well as the lurking terrors of existence. If universities do not give this kind of education, no other organizations will, unless it be theological colleges, many of which are now becoming admirably ecumenical in more ways than one.

And here we come to the essential point I want to make. Human beings will not be content to learn only about the means of life, will not be fobbed off with these no matter how ample they are. Men and women, in the midst of their predicaments, hunger to learn the meaning of life, and will turn to those who promise to tell them. One critic of the road along which universities are moving now sees education, in this large sense, passing "to the gurus of the mass media, the charismatic charlatans and sages, and the whole immense range of secular and religious street-corner fakirs and saints." This isn't really happening yet, but everyone can see the dangers. If we allow it to happen, we can forget about the advancement of knowledge and get ready to lament its decline. We need a public that respects knowledge, suspects the orthodox view, and supports the hunch that there is still something hidden behind the ranges. Lacking that, there will be neither the climate of opinion nor the resources needed for the advancement of knowledge. Those who are in too big a hurry for the advancement of knowledge may well defeat themselves.

Restoration of undergraduate teaching to parity, if not to primacy, will not be easy, because of the momentum of the opposing trend. It will require some reallocation of resources by universities, some improvement of the premiums offered for good teaching of undergraduates as against the premiums for other kinds of activity. These shifts cannot be made effectively by ukases from the top: they must gather very substantial support in the university community. If deans and heads of departments lack sympathy with such proposed shifts and are encouraged by their academic colleagues, they can delay indefinitely, and sometimes defeat, such shifts.

What stands in the way? Mainly the claims of original research and supervision of graduate students, creditable and honourable as I have already said. Honouring these claims at their present levels as bids for resources makes very large demands on the budgets. It makes even greater demands on individual staff members. At the prevailing staff-student ratios, which are not likely to be improved much in the immediate future, it is almost impossible for a member of staff to honour these claims at their present levels and also be a dedicated teacher of undergraduates. Something has to give way.

There has been much debate, mostly inconclusive, on the rival claims of undergraduate teaching versus postgraduate teaching and research in the universities in the last few years. For the most part, each side makes a good respectable case, and for this reason everybody shrinks from the hard decision about the best use of scarce resources. There is no time to rehearse all the issues here.

However, there are a few arguments I believe to have no substance, sacred cows standing across the path. I shall limit myself here to one sacred cow, or perhaps more correctly, to a cow just now going through the rituals that precede sanctification. It is being said, oftener and always with more emphasis, that one cannot be a good university teacher unless one carries along with his teaching a substantial commitment to research, that one can't keep alive in one's subject unless one is at work on the frontiers of knowledge where the excitement is. At the tenth quinquennial congress of the Universities of the Commonwealth in Australia recently I heard this proposition repeated again and again without serious challenge.

I have never believed it in the categorical way in which it is put forward, and none of the arguments for it have shaken my scepticism. To guard against misunderstanding, I must particularize. There may be subjects where it is true, but there remain many more where it is not. I do not argue the converse, that an able researcher cannot be a good teacher. Of course, many of them can and are, rich ornaments in any university. But not all able researchers can hold their passion for research and their duties in undergraduate teaching in the delicate balance that is called for. More important, indeed central for me, is a belief that many persons temperamentally suited, and capable of strong commitment, to teaching have no flair for, and little interest in, original research. I deplore their being told that they cannot be good teachers unless they are always sinking new shafts and mining new ore bodies. Central also is what we all know, that some very able researchers are indifferent, and even dreary, teachers. It is again a matter of bent, flair, temperament and interest about which we cannot do very much except to see it clearly and face the difficulties that have to be faced.

Naturally, no one can be a good teacher of anybody or anything unless he is vigorously alive in his subject. If it hasn't a surge of excitement for him, it certainly won't have for his students. But what teacher of what subject, if his bent is this way, will lack excitement in broadening his grasp of his subject, absorbing and digesting the

98

new knowledge that is being won on the frontier? Why any failure of stimulus, any sinking into boredom, while there are the innumerable links of his subject with other cognate subjects to be explored? How can it be dull to be thinking of the illumination that his subject, if it is worth teaching at all, throws on the whole human enterprise? A subject that is worth teaching and is taken in this way bristles with pedagogical problems: how to organize it so that its complexities yield to student effort, how to improve lucidity in exposition with the right words and the telling illustrations, how to design essay topics enabling the good student to march with him to the heights. Is there not here enough intellectual rigour, enough bait to keep curiosity alive, enough demand on a scholarly mind to last a lifetime? Of course there is, if one's bent is that way.

If it is said that there are not enough teachers or prospective teachers in sight with this kind of mind and bent, then universities should be hunting for them high up and low down, altering the postgraduate preparation required of those who aspire to university posts, hoping to draw out more of this kind of person and fewer of the would-be narrow specialists. When the universities find teachers of this kind of promise, they should surely be offering them more encouragement than they offer anyone else.

What I have set up here is not just a speculative model. There is supporting evidence: the best teachers I have known have worked on this model and given it nearly their whole effort, some perhaps sublimating a passion for research but most finding that research could not compare for fascination with teaching in the grand manner. Of course, my evidence is not massive enough for big generalizations. But the evidence for the proposition that good original research makes good teachers is partial too.

Sir Eric Ashby, Master of Clare College, Cambridge, who speaks cogently on the central issues that universities face in this period of rapid change, reassures me on the particular question before us. He said recently that one cannot be a first-class university teacher "without having regard to research," and then added in the same breath that this did not necessarily mean "doing research." "Having regard to research" does mean having respect for research findings, and particularly for the intellectual discipline and the techniques of research. It would include, in particular, scepticism of traditional and orthodox views in his subject, humility in the face of new evidence, suspension of judgement till all the available evidence is in, tentativeness in generalization until massive buttressing is found for it, eagerness to receive new and tested knowledge even when the teacher is not himself producing it. Finally, it means making manifest these attitudes and techniques to his students in his teaching. What more is needed for first-class teaching of undergraduates?

Research has become an honorific word in universities. Many of those who glorify it know more about research than they know about teaching. We need to think a lot more about the relation between research and teaching, which no doubt varies significantly from one subject to another. I hope there is enough provocation in what I have said to keep the debate going till all the available evidence is in. Nothing is more vital for the Canadian universities in the immediate future than careful decisions on this matter.

Lecture given at the University of British Columbia in January 1969. In 1966, the Duff-Berdahl Commission on University Government in Canada reported, recommending a larger share for members of teaching staffs in the governing of their universities. Following the report, most universities modified their constitutions in ways that conferred on teaching staffs, through faculty boards and senates, virtual control of academic policy. By the end of 1968 on several campuses, it appeared doubtful that teaching staffs would be able to agree how to exercise firmly and consistently the powers they had acquired.

Canadian Universities:
From Private Domain to Public Utility

The last decade has seen a remarkable physical expansion and change in Canadian universities. These developments were foreseen and were surprising only in the rapidity and relative effectiveness with which they were carried through. In the last two or three years, there has been a marked shaking up of their internal governments. The shake-up has not surpassed what was hoped for in some quarters, and feared in others, but was nevertheless surprising. Forecasts were wide of the mark. But the least foreseen and the most surprising change has been in the climate of opinion in which the universities operate, a shift from almost total public indifference about the universities and what they were doing or not doing to a widespread and almost breathless concern with what they are up to. Whether or not the fall of a sparrow in one of them is marked by God, it is heavily underlined by the mass media.

We are surprised, certainly; even yet, I think we do not fully comprehend. The shift has come quickly, its impact on the universities is not always visible to the naked eye; and, of course, the full impact is still to come. Indeed, for the long run this is the real revolution: not the change in scale, not the broadening of offerings, not the dominating by academic staff of the decisions that affect them vitally, not the rise of student power, not "participatory democracy" inside the university but participating democracy outside the university. The significant and permanent change is from the university as nobody's business to it as everybody's business.

We should not have been surprised at this change. Rather we should have been surprised that it did not happen sooner; that all, even the provincial universities, remained for so long quite outside the public domain, matters of essentially private concern. *Laissez-faire*, the philosophy of individualism and free private enterprise, ceased to have any significant restraining influence in this country at least a generation ago. Yet universities, true to dominant strains in their ancestry, reached the present decade as essentially private enterprises in their forms of organization, and in their ways of thinking and acting. Allowing for the inevitable divergences, the autonomous university has been the counterpart of the private corporation of fifty or a hundred years ago, deciding what products and services it would supply at the prices and standards it saw fit to set. University teachers, sometimes socialist in profession but always individualist in practice, fighting for, and usually winning, not only freedom of inquiry and freedom of expression, but also freedom to teach what they wanted in the ways they saw fit, have been in the individualist mould.

Laissez-faire, in other departments of life, has been replaced by collectivism, which is, in effect, the transfer of many decisions about your life and mine from you and me to big collectives, whether business corporations or trade unions or governments. Someone may say that the university itself is a collective that has been hedging him in on every side. So it is, but a very subordinate collective, as far as the big game of power is concerned, and perhaps for that reason, much the most permissive one I know about—a haven of individual freedom.

How did this subordinate collective manage to maintain its autonomy for so long, imposing only the lightest of yokes on its members? Because it rested in a backwater, out of the mainstream of life and action, little exposed to "the roar of bargain and battle." It touched directly only the lives of the tiny fraction of the young who became its students, roused the interest, and sometimes the concern, of their parents. In those who wanted to be its students and couldn't, it roused yearnings but not opposition or criticism.

It attracted almost no attention from general public opinion. It made little demand on governments, and was seen to assist in a modest way the implementing of urgent policies of government. I have often said before, and I say again because it is remarkable, that it is something of a tribute to Adam Smith's "invisible hand" that individuals pursuing their own private interest and advancement in securing an education made so effective a contribution to the common good. They manned the professions acceptably and improved the tone of life wherever they went.

That is to say, university education was serving the public interest with some effectiveness but in almost unnoticed ways. Entirely new dimensions of the public interest in higher education were taking shape in the 1950s and even earlier, but they too went almost unnoticed until the postwar generation of young people arrived at the doors of the universities. Then, many things suddenly became clear. The multiplying demand for higher education for the best of both public and private reasons, the great unfilled need, both public and private, for highly educated skills by a complex, highly organized society, the skyrocketing costs of meeting these demands and needs, and the immense governmental subsidies required to cover them, need no elaboration. It is enough to emphasize that university education has now joined the scramble at the public trough and is crowding other ravenous feeders there: health, welfare, highways, and so on, rousing envy, irritation and opposition.

The universities have moved into the public domain. Those who feel threatened by their hungry presence want to cut their pretensions and their costs. Those who expect direct benefits from universities, particularly governments, want to be assured that the directions they take will serve the beneficiaries most effectively, and with the least possible duplication of courses and effort. Not only costs, but content, organization, enrolment, kind and quality of service, are public issues. What case can the universities make to justify their continued autonomy? How do they have to behave to avoid such regulation?

Whatever the answer to these questions, some things are beyond question. The universities live on collective resources, assembled by governments from the taxpayer. So universities will have to serve the collective needs of the community. Who defines those collective needs and sets the priorities among them? That question is still open. Only this much can be said: unless the judgement of the university on collective needs and priorities, over a period of time, approaches the estimate of the government that pays the piper, then that government will call the tune. And the tune will be called conformably to the government's estimate of public opinion. What other course is open to a government dependent on public opinion?

Abject surrender by the universities is not by any means a foregone conclusion. In this game, they hold some high cards. "Knowledge is power" is a frayed cliché, but also a deep truth. Universities are more and more impressively every day the main repositories and dispensers of knowledge. Under proper nurture they can go on producing more and more new knowledge for which there is a limitless demand. So the universities, or to be more correct, their academic staffs, can put a price on their labours in the vineyard of knowledge, and so preserve things that public opinion would throw in the compost-heap. However, every university will have to have a firm consensus on the things it is determined to preserve, and stick to them resolutely and consistently. It will have to be accommodating on the range of offerings that serve the current conception of the public interest. Like other public utilities, it will have to seem to be serving acceptably what is called "public convenience and necessity." If any university wants to establish and hold a certain set of priorities, it will have to back them with a nearly unwavering common front.

That is to say, internal stability and unity is vital to the university retaining its autonomy in matters thought essential. Nations are as often destroyed from the inside as from the outside. In the last two or three years in most universities, the academics have constitutionalized the president's office, clinched their control of academic matters, and so got very powerful leverage on all important decisions. So powerful, in fact, that the president hesitates to act promptly and firmly in critical matters until he gets the academic nod. In substance, although not in form, *the members of the academic staff now have the main power*. This is an immensely significant change. *But they are not exercising it*. This is a fact of alarming portent. For the sake of internal stability and unity, they must now take firm positions. By discussion and compromise, they must agree to do what the president formerly did, or was charged with doing, by decree. The real enemy is not inside dictation from above any more. The potential enemies are internal dissension and indecision, and outside interference. Loyalty to one's discipline is an important professional commitment and defence. It grows stronger every day, but it must not displace loyalty to the integrity and stability of one's institution.

There will be plenty of pain in self-disciplined commitment to one's university. When cherished ambitions are voted down by one's colleagues, as they will be, and one can't revile the president any more to any effect, the temptation to revile one's colleagues for their obtuseness or malice will be severe. The model for disintegration and defeat is close to hand. The Nigerian tribes, having shaken off the British overlord, exhaust themselves in civil war.

Right now, careful thought and fairly quick decision by the main custodians of university power (academic staffs) are needed on what the university should be, and can be, after it has been discovered to be a public utility. What idea of the university has validity for those who have the power to say? Where is the citadel that must be defended, not merely to gratify the professors but in the long-run interests, as distinct from the short-run clamours, of the community? What can the garrison be roused to fight for in a united way?

It will not be possible to hold everything that has been held in the past. Decisions formerly made on inside preferences will have to take account also of outside needs. A substantial part of the available resources will have to be put into meeting collective needs, and so perhaps less into cherished projects of particular professors, departments and faculties. But it needn't be greatly less than in the past, when presidents and boards always had some sensitivity to collective needs. The main change is that it is no longer so much for presidents to decree as for academics to agree: not a big change in the substance of decisions to be taken, but a big shift in the responsibility for, and in the way of arriving at, decisions. Nor need there be any craven capitulation. Academic staffs have notable power and decisive influence in the important things if they do not dissipate them in indecision, suspended judgement, and internal division.

Exactly where is the citadel that must be defended? What is the cluster of essential functions and conventions that define the idea of the university and its mission in a way that *can* be defended for our time and circumstances? Generally speaking, it is whatever programme will draw and hold free minds, both inquiring and able, to its service, and they in turn will discover and educate other free minds for the service of our society and the larger world.

To this end, the university need not be utterly free in deciding all the subjects that will be taught. It can afford some concessions. But there are core subjects on which concessions cannot be made, mainly in mathematics, the sciences, social and humane studies, and the arts, because they are needed for central purposes. They are needed for conveying to students a grasp of the two cultures (in C. P. Snow's terms) and of the interrelations between them, for limbering up the mind, stirring up divine curiosity, giving muscle power to the intellect, sensitizing the creature to beauty, all in aid of understanding something of the mystery of man and his world. Not all students will want them all, but the feast should be there for the taking. These surely will be on nearly everybody's agenda as utter minima.

On the other hand, at the outer fringes there are many subjects that provide vocational skills and/or avocational frills but do not call for basic grounding in a group of the core subjects. These clearly should be the charge of the other postsecondary institutions of learning that are springing up. On these subjects at the fringe, there should be as stiff an exclusion policy as can be supported. In between the core and the periphery are many, many other subjects where delicate balancing of several considerations will be called for, such as the urgency of collective need for instruction in them, the quality of intellectual content in them, and the availability of other schools and agencies to give the instruction. These may not be attractive to inquiring, able, free minds, but should not be repulsive to such minds as long as they realize we live in an imperfect world.

Freedom in undertaking fundamental research should be much wider than in the subjects professed and taught. The instinct of governments and private corporations in research is likely to be predominantly utilitarian and short-run for the best of reasons for them: to get quick benefits in action to reassure taxpayers and shareholders. Fundamental research is usually a bigger gamble, but intelligent lunges into blank territory turn up spectacular results often enough to justify such gambles as can be afforded in support of persons with daring ideas and research flair.

There will be lots of false starts and final failures. The gambles should be undertaken where they have the best chances of success. The pay dirt is more likely to be struck where groups of explorers in interrelated disciplines are in close enough touch to get stimulus out of picking one another's brains. For the present, at any rate, this is most likely to happen oftenest in the universities.

In whatever is to be taught or researched, the minds engaged must be free, unhustled and uncircumscribed in their approach to the subject and in the detail of the content. No one presumes to instruct the doctors or the lawyers on the substance of the professional service they offer. The same respect must be tendered to the teaching and researching scholar if universities are to draw and hold the best people. Also, teachers and scholars must be protected in pursuing the truth as they see it, and in testifying to that truth at home or abroad. Here the interests of professor, university, and the larger community are at one. Because it is not always easy for elements of the public to see why, I shall say why, using words I have used before because I do not know how to say better something that needs to be said again and again.

The complex interdependent society in which we all live tends towards rigidities. Vested interests cluster round the *status quo*. They need to be shaken up from time to time by intelligent and perceptive criticism. This same society depends for its effectiveness on large-scale organizations, whether business corporations, trade unions, or governments, which tend to drag us all in their wake. Indeed, very large numbers of us are their employees: certainly, a very large bloc of the highly educated brainpower of the country is in their service, and the proportion will grow. Employees are inhibited from thoroughgoing, open criticism. But every *status quo* needs to be kept under critical review, even for its own good. Where are the free and knowledgeable critics to be found? Many of them will have to be found among the members of the academic staffs of the universities. Most of them will have to be educated in the universities where they learn the skills of critical analysis and intellectual integrity from the teachers who are not grinding anybody's axe. And how are such teachers to be drawn and held? Only, if at all, by ensuring freedom of thought and teaching.

I was careful *not* to say that teachers have to be utterly free in methods of teaching as distinct from content. The universities have been slacker about pedagogy than about scholarship, with unfortunate results. Much of the student unease about what is taught is at bottom a protest about how it is taught. Almost any subject can be made repellent by slipshod teaching. Academics have generally resisted their universities when review of the effectiveness of teaching was proposed, and perhaps they were right. But no free profession giving an indispensable public service can remain free to govern itself unless it establishes minimum professional standards for its members; and for teachers, standards that ensure respectable teaching skills must be set and met.

Anyway, with the internal shift in power, this matter, like many others, is now in the hands of the academics. Nothing will do so much to protect academic freedom as masterly and devoted teaching. Perhaps nothing less than good and devoted teaching will serve to hold student disaffection to manageable proportions.

This brings us to a question asked earlier: what can the garrison of the citadel of university autonomy, which, of course, includes the students, be roused to fight for in a united way? The academic staff will fight for academic freedom. So should the students. But why are numbers of them in a state of mutiny, acquiesced in, if not actively supported by, many others? It would be hard to know in the present confusion. Many reasons—some good, some bad; some understandable, some not. Some beyond the power of universities to deal with, no doubt. But some are within the power of the universities. Going on from what I hinted at a few minutes ago, I suggest more palatable food and a better balanced diet, not in the cafeteria but in the undergraduate classroom. If the food is better there, there will be less worry about it in the cafeteria.

In general, the balanced diet calls for more systematic teaching that bears on the meaning of life and evens up with the attention given to the means of life. Some would say more weight on broad general education, and less on highly specialized courses. I do not quite say that, because there is now so much specialized knowledge that bears on the meaning of life that to overlook it will turn classroom instruction into bull sessions. To take off into orbit for a wider view, one must have a launching pad. One must know, or at least have sensitive awareness of, much in particular if one is to make sense of things in general. At the same time, unless I am greatly misled, the thirst to understand as well as to know is stronger and afflicts more students now than in any recent past, and it is a noble affliction. The world he is going to have to live in doesn't make much sense to the reflective student, and for good enough reasons. He fairly asks the teacher of a specialty to give him some strong clues on the significance of that specialty for a larger prospect of man and his world. He fairly asks to be enabled to discover those unseen relationships that hopefully unite the professor's particulars to the particulars of other professors, and thence to a buttressed and more coherent view of the whole.

108

So, what is urged here is more systematic general education in breadth, groping for a synthesis of what we know, a synthesis wanted for living a full life and not merely for success in a specialized occupation. Because this general education needs buttressing, and at times correcting in detail, by the legitimate specialized studies, it should not get the higher priority I am urging at their expense. Because its main postulate is the unity of all knowledge and the indivisibility of truth, more systematic general education in breadth would help to correct, at times, presumption in some of the specialties. Because it affirms the central purpose of the university, it needs no other justification. What it would do to reduce disaffection in the student component of the garrison is a very important incidental benefit.

There is another potential threat to internal unity of the universities. They are largely engaged in teaching and research in the sciences and technology that serve the mass production apparatus of our economy. I myself think the universities have given somewhat too high a priority to this particular service. As I have just said, we give much study to the means of life and not enough to the meaning of life. We have got some of the priorities wrong. However, in some form or another, teaching and research in science and technology is one of the important collective needs of the community. Make no mistake about that. In preparing trained intelligence and technical skill and enlarging the knowledge at their command, the universities are not serving merely the great corporate structures, public and private. Essentially, they are staffing the structures that ensure the general affluence everybody has come to take for granted. If the universities suddenly abandoned their teaching and research in these fields, the pockets of poverty that everyone deplores would get bigger and deeper.

Beyond that altogether is the central consideration. The population continues to rise rapidly. There is universal thirst for still higher standards of living. This fact and this drive are the socio-economic forces that dominate political life and the thinking of politicians.

In one area after another, however, the uses now being made of science and technology dominate our lives, change, even pulverize, the social structure. In some respects, they work against rather than for a humane existence. We all know the evidence for saying, as forecast if not yet as fact, that technology is getting out of control.

We shall need much thought and effort to ensure that it is servant and not master.

More and more students are not only aware of the fly in the ointment but are bitter and resentful at the universities forging links that will bind us ever more tightly to what they think is an irresponsible science and a vagrant technology. The resentment is intensified by the spectacle of Vietnam where science and technology are used to add to the horrors and inhumanity of war. Although one must speak with caution about so irrepressibly vocal and volatile a movement, the more radical of these students now seem determined to force the universities to withdraw from the service of science and technology as inevitably corrupting influences, and then to use the institutions thus purified as bases for an assault on a corrupt society. As a first step in realizing this design, some students are now attempting to press universities to make official commitments of policy on disputed public issues; in substance, to align themselves with some sections of opinion against other sections of opinion.

Until the larger design unfolds still further, it is difficult to know whether to take all this seriously. Except on the assumption of recklessly revolutionary intentions, it seems a forlorn hope: even worse, a self-defeating project. Let us see why it looks that way. As I said earlier, the pressure of population and the universal demand for a higher standard of living really set the objectives of all political parties. Those who push the universities to drop their support of teaching and research in utilitarian science and technology (basic community needs) are trying to use dependent and politically weak institutions to fight the most powerful political forces in the community. As Emerson said long ago, "If you shoot at a king, you must kill him." Students cannot win the big game against the allegedly corrupt society with these weapons and this strategy.

For the sake of argument, let us assume that they succeed in diminishing the effectiveness of the utilitarian service provided by the knowledge industry in the universities. Their most hated enemy, the big industrial corporations, would suffer the least. They have the resources, if need be, to do their own research and educate their own scientists. The serious sufferers would be small industry and small business which can't afford to grow their own scientists and run their own research, and of course, the people on the poverty line who are first in peril if the national income declines.

The one certain achievement of the success assumed here would

110

be destruction of the autonomy of the universities. They cannot survive in freedom if they, as institutions, deliberately flout the dominant political forces in the community. When they lose their autonomy, the only sure protection of freedom of inquiry and freedom of teaching for individual staff members would be lost too. The only indispensable members of the university community are the persons who value these freedoms and will speak their minds at whatever cost. Making them vulnerable will debase the universities still further.

There are many ways of undermining academic freedom. One sure method is for universities to abandon their neutrality on disputed public issues and officially take positions on the side of the angels. Of course, members of academic staffs, as individuals, must be free to speak their minds on all public issues whether on the side of the angels or not. It would be hard to find now a university where they are not free to do so. But the price of their freedom to do so is the strict official neutrality of the university itself. If the university declares a policy on public issues, it makes itself ridiculous if it tolerates teachings and opinions by members of its staff contrary to its policy. And where will it stand with a government from which it draws its lifeblood in the form of grants when that government's policy runs counter to the policy the university has espoused?

Reasonable requests made by students should be met, and meeting them will help to unify the university community in defence of its autonomy and in defence of freedom of inquiry and teaching. But concessions to extremist demands that are disruptive in consequence if not in aim, weaken the university and throw doubt on its capacity to order its own affairs. If doubt of this capacity deepens, there will be outside interference. Members of university staffs who want to go on working in the universities in conditions of freedom have the most to lose from this outcome. Equally, they are the people who can determine the outcome. The power conferred by knowledge is in their hands. If they don't organize to use it for protecting the autonomy of the universities, they will lose it. Power always expires in a vacuum.

It is vital to get some things clear. Much of the substance of power has been taken out of the president's office and away from the board of governors. The members of the academic staff now have what has been taken out, and they have nearly a veto on the use of what is left. They may find this hard to believe, but it is true. *That battle is over*. But those who have newly won power are not exercising what they have. On many campuses, the extremist radicals among the students are trying to seize it. But they can't take from the hands of the president and his senior officers what isn't there. If they are to take it, they must take it from where it is—from the members of the academic staff.

Of course, faculty boards and senates are debating assemblies, by tradition and instinct. Debating assemblies, except where led by a strong executive, are much better at delaying and restraining power than they are at exercising it. Failing firm decision and action inside, there will be interference from the outside. Direct and pervasive control by governments will come, not because governments want it, but because they, like nature, abhor a vacuum.

Convocation address at the University of New Brunswick, October 1969. Through the period 1967–1969 activist student attack on the government of universities, reformed or unreformed, treated the universities as if they were political entities to which the principles and theories of political democracy could be fully applied. This assumption had never been subjected to close analysis. Nor had any attention been paid to an important maxim of practical wisdom applicable to organizations of every kind: that power should always be related to function and run hand in hand with responsibility.*

University Government

For several years now, we have debated strenuously about the government of Canadian universities. Many think they have been governed on the wrong principle but don't agree on the right principle. Some think they are governed too much, others that they are not governed enough. In all this, almost nobody speaks up for the way they were governed until yesterday. The formal structure of university government was sufficiently autocratic in appearance to offend deeply the rising and vocal classes, the teaching staff and the students.

In most universities until yesterday, all final legal authority rested with the board of governors on the model of the absolute monarch, or with the president and the board on the model of the commercial corporation. In governing structures anywhere, the reality rarely follows the forms closely. This formal absolutism was much softened in practice in most places by the convention that in academic matters the board either delegated authority to the president or acted only on his advice. He, in turn, usually did not act or recommend until he was satisfied of pretty solid support in the teaching staff.

*Published in Queen's Quarterly, LXXVI, No. 4 (Winter 1969).

However, there was, in most universities, enough intervention by boards of governors in critically important academic matters to upset the teaching staff. They rightly objected to laymen intervening in issues which they had no competence to judge. Then, with some forensic licence, they assembled their grievances and laid them all at the door of a bungling, if not perverse, board of governors and a president thought always to be at the bidding of the board. This overstated the case considerably. On top of all this, the teaching staff asserted a principle. The university is essentially a community of scholars, equal in concern for their common life as scholars, even if not equal in rank. This community should be a self-governing community. If there are to be boards of governors, they must either be controlled by scholars or limited to very narrow functions.

As this case was being developed, students were understandably finding defects in the service the university was giving them. They made no distinction between what could be cured quickly and what would have to be endured in a time of rapid expansion, cramped financing, critical shortage of competent staff, and so on. They laid it all at the door of the so-called arbitrary government of the university. The more radical of them added another count in the indictment. The university should be carrying the banner of general social reform. It was prevented from doing so by a reactionary board of governors who were grimly binding it to the service of the established *status quo*.

There is little evidence that the radical students who have led the debate thought things would be improved by giving power to the professors, but they did pick up the professors' idea of the self-governing community, proclaimed their membership in it, and then adapted the idea to their purposes. The students, the radicals say, are the important members of the university community, the persons for whom the whole show is organized. The university is, they imply, a consumers' cooperative, and the producers should not dominate it. The scholars' aristocratic republic is not for them.

For the most part, the radical activist students do not think of themselves as scholars in embryo, but as men of action now, whose concerns go beyond scholarship if not away from it. They want the university to be a popular democracy. In such a democracy, there is no place of special privilege for an élite board of governors or a haughty aristocracy of scholars. All there should be is participatory democracy by all members of the self-governing community.

114

The theoreticians in the activist student movement adopted for their purposes the rhetoric of democratic politics. They apply to the university all the arguments we accept for governing any one of the ten provinces and the Canadian federation. Everybody should share in the decisions that affect everybody. If everybody can't be there in person, he should be there through his chosen representative. We haven't yet heard the final argument of representative democratic government, namely that each constituency should be represented according to population. If we are patient and wait, we will hear it.

We shall hear more than that. If the university is really a political organization in which demands for democracy in the fullest political sense are appropriate, there are still other constituencies to be heard from. To be specific, every university has a sizeable operating staff that keeps up a flow of essential services of various kinds for students and scholars. (For convenience of reference, I shall call them housekeepers.) Many of them give a lifetime of service to their university. If everybody who is affected by decisions should share in governing, it will be hard to find reasons for excluding the housekeepers. Students are here today and gone tomorrow. A significant proportion of the teaching staff is here today and gone the day after tomorrow. How can they claim a big share in governing while long-service servants of the university are denied it? This question is beginning to be asked.

If students and teaching staff have a democratic right to sit on the governing body determining questions of finance and housekeeping, surely the housekeepers who have an interest in finance as well as housekeeping should be there too. Equally, on democratic principle, housekeepers have as good a claim to share in academic decisions as have staff and students to share in housekeeping decisions.

A theory that does not keep power and authority closely tied to function should be looked at very carefully. Is the university really a political community to which the principles of democratic politics can be applied wholesale? This is what I want to examine.

First, a cautionary point more practical than theoretical. A community that proposes to govern its own life in a thoroughgoing way needs a very large control over the means needed to sustain its life. If many of these means are in the hands of bodies outside itself, it is to that degree a subordinate, dependent community. Insofar as it lacks self-sufficiency, severe limits are put on its self-governing capacity. For sheer self-preservation, it has to shape its government so that it always has friends in the courts of its patron, the political government of the day.

Universities are increasingly dependent on provincial governments. Most of the plans for drastic reform of university government have ignored this brute fact. The insistence on self-government has sharpened even as dependence on outside authorities has deepened. Such insistence is understandable as an emotional reflex as the lengthening shadow of governments darkens the sky. We would all like to escape into the light of freedom, but beating the drum for full self-government is not a rational response when we must go on pressing governments for still larger means.

Second, and more fundamental to the theory we are examining, the university is a voluntary association. No one is required to belong to it or give it his allegiance. He can leave it at a moment's notice without penalty if he finds its yoke irksome. The situation is far different with membership in the truly political community which we call the state.

No one can escape the clutches of the state merely by resigning or announcing that he quits. To escape, he must leave the country with all the tearing up of roots that attends his leaving. And no matter where he goes, he will be at the mercy of another state. As long as he stays, his resignation is ineffective. The state will impose taxes on him that he must pay, make and enforce laws that he must obey, on pain of punishment. The state has a monopoly of coercive power which can break us utterly. Small wonder, then, that men fought grimly for a share of power, through representatives of their choosing, for a voice in the levying of taxes and the making of laws!

Democratic theory and practice were fashioned for bringing the awesome coercive power of the state under control. The full logic of democracy is convincing only in the realm of the state, in the truly political community. Transferring it to the realm of university government is a kind of hocus-pocus, dressing up a sheep in the skin of a lion.

Third, democratic politics, wherever practised, exacts a price that we must pay. Where the representatives of divergent and conflicting interests meet and have to reach a decision by majority vote, the result is nearly always a compromise that almost nobody likes except the fellows who get their main satisfaction out of negotiating the compromises. This is not the time or place to consider why this is so and is likely to remain so for a long time. It will enforce the

116

point enough if we remind ourselves that while nearly everybody cheers for democracy almost nobody thinks very highly of the results. As Winston Churchill said, "Democracy is the worst form of government, except all the others that have been tried." Nearly everybody reviles political parties, abuses politicians, and speaks contemptuously of legislatures because what they do is nobody's first best, but nearly always their second best, or third best, or almost intolerable. That is to say, the decisions that come out of the democratic process of compromise are often tainted with mediocrity. We accept them, pay the price for order and peace, but we should not use all this apparatus of representation, long discussion, voting and compromise where it is not needed. We ought to keep as many activities as we can free of compromise where the persons involved are free to do their best in the way they think best, without everybody having a say about everything.

Uninhibited teaching, unhurried thought and reflection, undistracted probing of the mysteries on the frontiers of knowledge, the main work of a university, require freedom from compromise more than almost any other of our enterprises. We know this from long experience.

Among those who have given their lives to it and know what they are talking about, there is little disagreement about the objectives of the university, although there are always some differences about priorities among these objectives. That is to say, there is much more unity on purposes in the university than there is among voters in a provincial election. There is much less diversity of clashing interests than there is in the Canadian federation.

Of course, there have to be some compromises in settling priorities in the university, but the compromising will be greatly increased rather than eliminated by turning the university into a political arena where factions and organized parties contend for votes and majorities.

Log rolling for the purpose of making majorities and other political manoeuvres are fun, and some people are better at it than others. But there is no evidence that the best manoeuvrers have the strongest grip on principle and overriding purposes. Anyway, zest for the game tends to obscure principle and purpose, and to make the game an end in itself.

Factions contending over the policy of a university will give governments and public the impression that the university does not know how to run its affairs, and the temptation for governments to intervene and set policy will become almost irresistible. So, the high-minded students who hate compromise are likely to incur the very thing they hate most. Applying the full logic of political democracy to the governing of the university must end by debasing it.

I add quickly that all the homely virtues of the democractic spirit have a vital place in it. A procedure for hearing grievances, the most anxious attention given to representations put forward in a reasonable spirit, a scrupulously honoured practice of widespread consultation are utterly essential. They will do more than anything else to make a harmonious community of students and scholars, and to firm up a consensus which ostracizes those who will not play the game in this spirit.

Still, authority in the university must be shown to be legitimate. Just because it has become suspect, it must show valid title deeds. The principle for this display is easy enough: authority must be related to function. Functions must be defined, and competence for them must be manifest. This is the sure way to restore the order and respect that are now threatened, to show that there is no need for everybody to be involved in deciding everything.

The function of a board of governors is to conserve the property and enlarge the means of the university, to oversee its financial operations and housekeeping, and to maintain liaison with governments and the general public. Indeed, its one indispensable function is to maintain the confidence of the public and the relevant governments in the way the university is run, and to defend in those quarters the essential freedom of the university in its work. It would be better if it were called a board of trustees because its job is to hold the university in trust rather than to govern its manifold operations.

For these reasons, the board of trustees, as I shall now call it, should be a predominantly lay body. If some representation of staff and students will serve to allay fears and scotch rumours of wicked doings in its councils, well and good. Putting the final authority in a board made up of staff and students would not maintain public confidence. For a long time yet, it must be recognized that the large public (to which governments always respond in the long run) resents the privileged position of students and doubts the practical wisdom of professors. Enough evidence is always emerging somewhere to keep that doubt alive. And the public does not readily appreciate the larger wisdom for the long run that often comes from reflection undistracted by the practical urgencies of the short run.

Of course, the laymen on a board of trustees have no sure competence in academic matters that they can put up against the members of the academic staff. It must be made clear by law or settled understanding that they do not intervene in academic matters. Within the limits that finance makes possible, the board must delegate to, or accept the recommendations of, the president.

Teaching staffs everywhere are now being confirmed in virtual control of academic matters. The senate, which speaks for them, must coordinate and integrate academic policy, thus virtually compelling the board and president to accept its recommendation in all but the most unusual circumstances. These changes are now well advanced. They are right and proper. They will make the academic staff as much of a self-governing community as the world is likely to put up with.

Whatever part students are to have in governing must also be related to function and status, and to the legitimate interests students have in the educational process. The small groups of rebellious students are scornful of token representation. The political parallels they draw are designed to get them eventual control of the governing bodies. Nothing in the function, status or interests of the students entitles them to that power.

Their function in the university is to be learners, not operators, to learn in a short period free of distractions what they can never learn anywhere else—a full-time job. They are here today and gone tomorrow, and they do not possess enough knowledge and experience to justify the entrusting of power to transients. Even if King Solomon appeared as a visiting professor, they themselves would object to his having power in university decisions. Then, aside altogether from status and function, their presence in any numbers on the board of trustees will not help to maintain the confidence of governments and the public—quite the reverse. So it should be tokenism or nothing, as far as representation on board and senate are concerned.

Status and function do justify self-government by students of their extracurricular activities, the control of all student discipline except academic discipline. They can fairly claim to govern, and run if they want to, the ancillary services they require and for which they pay. But nothing said so far provides for protection of the student's deepest interest—anxious attention by the university to the educational opportunity offered him. However far student disaffection wanders off this issue at times, this is still its heart. The extremes of rebellion and violence would not have been tolerated by the moderate students—perhaps would not have been a problem at all—if the universities had been doing their job of education well in this period of rapid expansion.

The extremes have emerged partly because most universities are engaged in some activities they should not be in at all, but mainly because some legitimate activities have been overemphasized, allowed to take priority over teaching of high quality, teaching that does justice to broad general education as well as to abstruse specialties. There is no chance that rebellion and disaffection will end until the priorities are overhauled. The members of the self-governing community of scholars will have to realize that they are teachers first, abstruse specialists, researchers, and consultants afterwards.

In most universities now, too many members of staff give lip service to the priority of teaching but do not really honour it. Accordingly, student pressure on the universities should be continued, as no doubt it will. The proper channels for the pressure are organs of consultation, advisory committees, student membership on committees that consider curriculum, and access to committees that recommend on tenure and promotion, places where those who know how the shoe pinches can be heard.

I have sketched the outlines of the model for university government that I would urge. The model tries to relate authority to function. It persuades me that the existing structure of two-tier government through board of trustees and senate, with some modifications, will best serve the well-ordered university. It makes it unnecessary for everybody to have a hand in deciding everything.

However, as we know well, the two-tier system is under severe criticism, being blamed wrongly for most of our present troubles. In fact, some universities are now thinking that the troubles call for drastic surgery, replacing the two-ventricle heart with a one-ventricle —a one-tier governing body consisting of roughly equal numbers of lay persons, academic staff, and students. There are significant differences between universities, and for some this may be the least of the evils within which they must choose. At the same time, there are dangers that should be looked at very carefully.

If the one-tier governing body is big enough to be genuinely representative of all constituencies, can it be kept small enough to be an effective body for debating high policy instead of becoming a forum for haranguing the multitude? Authority, in this instance voting power, will not be determined by function and status. Will such a

120

one-tier government allow enough influence in complex issues to those who are best informed about them? Isn't the one-tier structure likely to institutionalize the very thing the academics resent and fear, intrusion of lay members in academic decisions they are not competent to make? This is not fanciful: it is a very real danger—in the short run. And it is the short run that matters when you are trying to establish the legitimacy of a new form of government.

Until the universities adjust some priorities more favourably to the teaching function, the tensions between academic staff and students will continue to rise. Students who are dissatisfied, but not openly rebellious (and I believe there are many more of these than we think), are finding out that the main obstacle to the adjustments they want is not the obscurantist lay board of governors, not the much reviled president and his senior officers, but the academic staff.

In the one-tier structure, the students will quickly find out that the readjustments that are possible in finance, budgeting and housekeeping are relatively minor—minor at any rate until adjustments in academic policy are made. So the big contention will be over academic policy, with representatives of teachers and students on opposite sides on very important issues. Insofar as these two groups are roughly equal in numbers, the balance of power will likely be held by the lay membership. In these circumstances, how are the lay members to avoid becoming the arbiters of academic policy? This would be a strange finale for a movement that all began as the dream of a self-governing community of scholars!